Bridge Made Easy

Book One
Elementary

A Simple Explanation
of Scientific Bidding
and a Dozen of the Most
Important Card Plays

by Caroline Sydnor

Published by
Devyn Press, Inc.
3600 Chamberlain Lane, Suite 230
Louisville, KY 40241
1-800-274-2221
Fax 502-426-2044

See the back cover for ordering in...

P9-CDX-701

First Printing, May 1975
Second Printing, December 1975
Third Printing, January 1978
Fourth Printing, December 1980
Fifth Printing, December 1983
Sixth Printing, February 1986
Seventh Printing, February 1988
Eighth Printing, September 1990
Ninth Printing, October 1993
Tenth Printing, November 1996
Eleventh Printing, July 2004

ISBN #0-939460-79-3

Dedicated to Winnie Fuerbringer and Frankie Welch, who encouraged me, and to my students, who taught me how to teach.

Former President Gerald Ford accepts a copy of **Bridge Made Easy** *from the author. Betty Ford says her husband is "the bridge player in the family."*

Photo by Craig
© 1975

and the side playing the highest card wins the trick and the right to lead to the next trick. The Ace will take any trick in its suit, the King is the next highest, then the Queen, Jack, 10, 9, etc. There are 13 tricks.

The person who wins the bidding, called the declarer, must take a "book" of six tricks before he can start counting for his contract. If he bid 1 Spade he must take his book of six and then one . . . 6 + 1 = 7 tricks. If he bid 4 Spades he needs 6 + 4 = 10 tricks.

The player who first bid the denomination of the final contract is the "declarer". The player on his left has the privilege of playing the first card, called leading. It is good strategy for him to study his cards to see which suit might bring in the most tricks for his side and lead a card from that suit. Then the play proceeds clockwise around the table until each has played a card. You must play a card in the suit that is led if you have one.

CONTENTS

PLAYS DESCRIBED

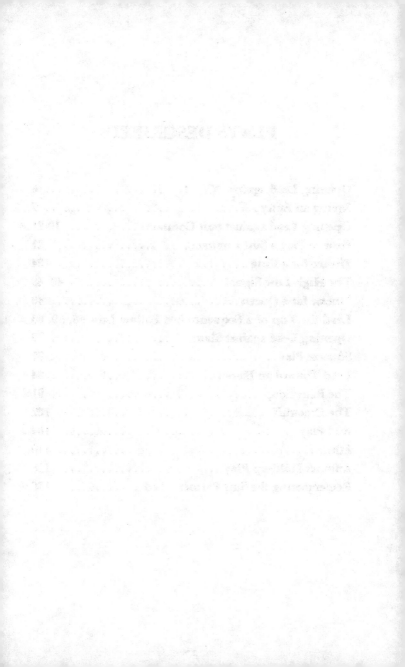

I. NO TRUMP BIDDING AND PLAY

There is an easy way to evaluate your hand at bridge, if you use the point-count method which assesses high cards on their trick-taking strength.

Ace .... 4 points
King .... 3 points
Queen .... 2 points
Jack .... 1 point

That's a total of 40 points in the deck and 10 points make an average hand.

You want to learn how to tell your partner how many points you have and where they are by making a bid that describes your holding, or you can tell him you have few or none by passing. Similarly, you want your partner to picture his hand to you. Here's how it works. Suppose you dealt a hand and your cards were:

♠ AQ72   ♥ A63   ♦ A62   ♣ KJ4

You dealt yourself a very fine hand, 18 high-card points, almost half the deck, and your points and your cards are evenly distributed among the four suits. With this hand you would open the bidding with 1 No Trump.

It's the most descriptive bid in bridge and has reached near-perfection in carrying information to your partner. The bid says, "I have specifically 16 to 18 high-card points, no more and no less, a balanced hand,

and three of the four suits are protected."

A balanced hand is one in which the cards are evenly divided among the four suits. It cannot have a void (no cards in one suit), a singleton (only one card in a suit), and can have only one doubleton. Therefore, the distribution can be 4-3-3-3, 4-4-3-2, or 5-3-3-2. Here are some examples:

♠Q543	♥KJ3	♦A98	♣AQ4
♠KQ73	♥AK62	♦982	♣AQ
♠Q4	♥AQ7	♦Q86	♣AK952

A suit that is protected has a card that can take a trick, an Ace, a King, or a Queen. The Queen should have two little cards with it, one to follow to the Ace and one to follow to the King so you'd still have the Queen left to win the third round.

If you have a doubleton one of the two cards should be a big one, the Ace, the King, or the Queen. Otherwise, it is considered a worthless doubleton and risky in a No Trump contract.

Responses to 1 No Trump

After you bid 1 No Trump the bidding proceeds clockwise around the table. When it's your partner's turn, he will tell you what his hand is like by making a bid or by passing.

His answer is based on whether he sees any hope

for a game, which is 3 No Trump. That takes 26 high-card points in the two hands added together. Your partner will count his hand and add his total to your 16-17-18 points. It's simple arithmetic.

Let's move you around the table and let you respond to the opening 1 No Trump. With 0 to 7 points you will pass. Even if the opener is on the top of his bid there's no game, $7+18=25$.

With 8 or 9 points you aren't sure. You bid 2 No Trump inviting your partner to go to game if he has 17 or 18 points. If he has the minimum of 16 your partner will decline the invitation by passing.

With 10 to 14 points you see game even if your partner is on the bottom of his bid, $10 + 16 = 26$. You jump to 3 No Trump.

On this hand your cards are:

♠KJ5　　♥84　　♦J84　　♣AQ876

That's 11 + your partner's 16=27. You jump to 3 No Trump. You see game and you bid it.

The Play of the Hand

The declarer is the one who first called No Trump. His left-hand opponent has the privilege of making the opening lead. Then declarer's partner neatly puts his cards face up on the table, because he will be the "dummy". The declarer gets to see his partner's hand, a great advantage, and gets to play his partner's cards as well as his own.

Flash Card

1 No Trump ☐	Pass with 0-7
	Bid 2 NT with 8-9
	Bid 3 NT with 10-14

shows
16-18 points
even distribution
3 suits protected

1. Opening 1 NT Drill

1. Can you open 1 NT on these hands? If not, why?
Figure the high card points.

♠ AKQ	♠ AK2	♠ AK2	♠ K4
♥ K93	♥ 963	♥ 5	♥ K7
♦ QJ4	♦ QJ4	♦ QJ432	♦ AK963
♣ KJ96	♣ AQ32	♣ AK72	♣ KJ65

2. Your partner opened 1 NT. What is your response?
point count?

♠ 1072	♠ Q32	♠ A82
♥ AJ8	♥ KQ4	♥ KJ4
♦ J54	♦ J72	♦ Q432
♣ 9743	♣ 7532	♣ 952

3. The bidding went: You   Partner
                         1 NT [ ]   2 NT
                          ?

What's your rebid?

♠ K4	♠ KQ4	♠ A72
♥ A765	♥ KJ76	♥ KQ87
♦ K987	♦ A7	♦ K76
♣ AQ8	♣ KQ94	♣ KQ3

4. What is your lead against 3 NT?

♠ QJ1072	♠ Q10862	♠ KQJ72
♥ A72	♥ KJ4	♥ J108743
♦ 765	♦ 853	♦ 9
♣ 32	♣ 65	♣ 4

1. Bidding 1 No Trump

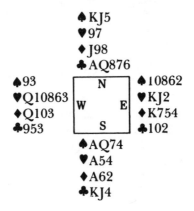

                    ♠ KJ5
                    ♥ 97
                    ♦ J98
                    ♣ AQ876

    ♠ 93   N   ♠ 10862
    ♥ Q10863   ♥ KJ2
    ♦ Q103   W   E   ♦ K754
    ♣ 953   S   ♣ 102

                    ♠ AQ74
                    ♥ A54
                    ♦ A62
                    ♣ KJ4

South deals
The bidding:

SOUTH	WEST	NORTH	EAST
1 NT	Pass	3 NT	Pass
Pass	Pass		

The Opening Lead

In a No Trump contract, the side that sets up its long suit first usually wins the hand, so the opening leader plays a card from his longest and strongest suit. If he has a sequence of three honors (honors are Ace, King, Queen, Jack, 10) he leads the top of it; otherwise, he leads the fourth best card counting from the top. For example:

KQJ72   J10962   KJ872   AJ94

So West led the 6 of Hearts. From dummy declarer played low (second hand usually plays low) and East played his best Heart (third hand usually plays high). East's best is a beautiful card, the King, and East feels sure the No Trump bidder has the Ace and will capture his King, but he played it anyway, sacrificing it to set up cards in his partner's hand. Declarer laid down the Ace, won the trick and the right to lead next.

Declarer's Play

Silently South added the two hands together counting his tricks. Spade AKQJ = four, Heart A = one, Diamond A = one, Club AKQJ and maybe the 8 = four or five. Total = ten or eleven. He chose to play his best suit first, Clubs.

Save an Entry

When you are planning to run a long suit, you carefully save an entry to the hand which has the most cards in that suit.

♣AQ876

♣KJ4

Dummy was longer in Clubs and declarer's hand was shorter in Clubs. He cashed the big cards in the short hand first, saving the little card as an entry to the long hand.

South played the King, then the Jack of Clubs, and

the 4 was the entry to dummy where he took the Ace and Queen.

Declarer counted the Clubs as they fell. The opponents had played all theirs so the 8 of Clubs was high. He cashed it. It was *No* Trump so no one could trump it.

It was wise of South to take all the Club tricks at one time so he wouldn't forget they were winners.

Now South moved to his next best suit, Spades. It illustrated the same principle. He played the King, then the Jack, now a small one to enter his hand to cash the Ace and Queen. This long-hand short-hand maneuver is simple, but it is fundamental to good card play.

The Ace of Diamonds was his eleventh and last trick. East got in with the King of Diamonds and led a Heart to his partner who won the final trick with the Heart Queen.

When a player is unable to follow suit, he is careful to discard (to throw away) useless cards. East saved his King and a small Diamond to protect it and a Heart to return his partner's suit.

East and West are married to the suit of the opening lead and play it at every opportunity. On this hand the opportunity came too late. Alas, they had four good Heart tricks but couldn't get in the lead soon enough to get all of them.

Scoring

In scoring No Trump, the first trick (after the book of six tricks) is worth 40 and each after that 30.

It takes 100 below the line to make a "game". The first side scoring two games wins a "rubber" and a big bonus.

On this hand you bid 3 NT and made it plus two overtricks.

It's *Contract* Bridge: everything contracted for goes below the line and everything not contracted for goes above the line. Draw a wavy line to denote a game won. Here's the score for the first hand.

We	They
60	
100	

There is a deck of cards that will deal quickly this identical hand, and all the other hands in *Bridge Made Easy, Book One*.

For the deck to work, the deal must rotate as it does in regular bridge. South deals hand 1, automatically receiving the cards printed in the South hand above. West deals hand 2, North hand 3, and East hand 4. Thus it follows throughout.

(To order cards see back cover.)

2. Partner Invites Game

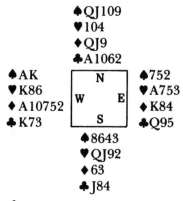

♠QJ109
♥104
♦QJ9
♣A1062

♠AK   ♠752
♥K86   ♥A753
♦A10752   ♦K84
♣K73   ♣Q95

♠8643
♥QJ92
♦63
♣J84

West deals
The bidding:

WEST	NORTH	EAST	SOUTH
1 NT	Pass	2 NT	Pass
3 NT	Pass	Pass	Pass

West had 17 points and opened one No Trump. East had 9 points and wasn't sure the partnership had enough for game. He bid two No Trump inviting his partner to go to game if West was on the top of his bid. West had 17 points so he accepted.

North led the top of his sequence in honors, the Queen of Spades.

Deciarer counted his winners. Spade AK = two, Heart AK = two, Diamond AK = two, Club K or Q = one. That was only seven tricks. He looked for the best place to develop two more tricks. It was in the long Diamond suit.

West won the first trick with the Spade King and attacked his long suit right away, leading a low Diamond to the King. He led a low Diamond back and ducked, allowing North to win the Jack.

North pursued Spades with the Jack. Declarer took the Ace. Now West cashed the Diamond Ace and counted 11 Diamonds played. His two Diamonds were the only ones remaining so he collected the Diamond 10 and 7.

He switched to a Club to set up an honor and North won his Ace. North's Spades were high, so he took the Spade 10 and the 9, and then led the Heart 10. Declarer collected his King of Hearts, Ace of Hearts, and his good Club, making his contract for nine tricks.

3. Playing One No Trump

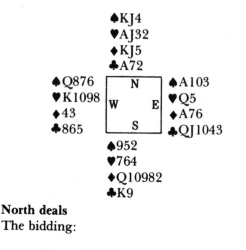

♠KJ4
♥AJ32
♦KJ5
♣A72

♠Q876
♥K1098
♦43
♣865

♠A103
♥Q5
♦A76
♣QJ1043

♠952
♥764
♦Q10982
♣K9

North deals
The bidding:

NORTH	EAST	SOUTH	WEST
1 NT	Pass	Pass	Pass

North had a No Trump opener but South couldn't help. With only five points there was no chance for game and he passed.

East led the Club Queen. North paused to count his winners: Spade K = one maybe, Heart A = one, Diamond QJ109 = four, Club AK = two. That was seven sure tricks and one probable.

North picked up the Club trick in his own hand saving the King in dummy in case he needed it to get to his long Diamond suit. He laid down the Diamond King and East ducked.

Declarer continued the Diamond Jack and again East ducked. East was hoping to kill declarer's entry to the Diamond suit but declarer had another Diamond and he led it and East had to take it with the Ace.

East returned a Club to dummy's King. Now declarer ran the two good Diamonds in dummy. Then he led a low Spade. West followed low, declarer inserted the Jack, and East had to go up with the Ace.

Now East took his three good Clubs. Then he played a Heart and declarer won it with his Ace and took the last trick with his Spade King, making an overtrick.

4. Playing Two No Trump

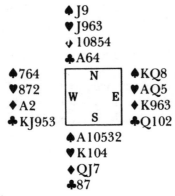

```
              ♠ J9
              ♥ J963
              ♦ 10854
              ♣ A64
  ♠ 764         N        ♠ KQ8
  ♥ 872                  ♥ AQ5
  ♦ A2      W     E      ♦ K963
  ♣ KJ953      S         ♣ Q102
              ♠ A10532
              ♥ K104
              ♦ QJ7
              ♣ 87
```

East deals
The bidding:

EAST	SOUTH	WEST	NORTH
1 NT	Pass	2 NT	Pass
Pass	Pass		

East started with one No Trump and West invited game with 8 points, but East had a minimum hand and passed.

South led the Spade 3, the fourth best of his long suit. East studied his winners: Spade K = one, Heart A and the Queen maybe = one or two, Diamond AK = two, Club QJ109 = four. Total of eight or nine.

North played "third hand high", the Spade Jack, and declarer won the Spade Queen. He led the Queen of Clubs, starting to set up his longest suit. North hopped up with the Club Ace to return the 9 of Spades. Declarer played the 8, but South overtook North's 9 with his 10 and laid down the Ace. The King fell and South picked up two more Spade tricks. The defenders were book-in, and declarer needed all the rest.

South exited with the Diamond Queen which was won with dummy's Ace. Now East ran his long suit playing a low Club to the 10, and the 2 back to the King, Jack and 9. Then he led a Heart to the Ace and took the good King of Diamonds making his 2 No Trump.

The Score

The score for these four hands as played in the textbook looked like this . . .

We (NS)	They (EW)
③ 30	
① 60	
① 100	
	100 ②
③ 40	70 ④

Tips:

Any time any part of your body is touching the table someone can see your cards.

Tricks are stacked neatly so everyone can count them easily. Declarer picks up his own tricks and after winning his first six slides them together in a "book". Then stacks his others separately.

Book

and five

The defender who picks up the first trick for his side should take up the others for his side for that hand.

II. BIDDING ONE SPADE OR ONE HEART

When you pick up a new hand the first thing you look for is an opening bid of 1 No Trump.

♠ AK94   ♥ AQ762   ♦ 8   ♣ AJ9

On this hand the point count is 18, three of the suits are protected, but the distribution isn't even. It would be a foolish risk to play this at No Trump. The opponents might ruin you with Diamond leads.

However, this type of hand is excellent in a suit contract. If you won the auction with a Heart contract, you could "trump" those Diamonds. You would follow to the Ace, but when the King was led, you wouldn't have any more, so you could trump it with a Heart. The smallest trump outranks the biggest Diamond. So at a suit contract you get extra points for uneven distribution:

> Void .... 3 points
> Singleton .... 2 points
> Doubleton .... 1 point

Now count your hand again. It's worth 20 points.

When you open the bidding with 1 Spade or 1 Heart, you show a five-card suit and between 13 and 21 points, counting both your high cards and your distribution. You also promise two and one-half quick tricks. A quick trick is a card expected to win a trick in the first or second round of play of a suit:

> AK = 2   A = 1   Kx = ½
> AQ = 1½   KQ = 1

That describes this hand, so you bid 1 Heart.

Required for Game

It takes 4 Hearts to make a game. That's 10 tricks. To take that many, you need 26 points and eight or more cards in the trump suit.

Partner's Response

In order to raise you to 2 Hearts, your partner needs 6 to 10 points and three of your suit to guarantee eight trumps.

He can give you a double raise and jump to 3 Hearts with 13 to 15 points and four trumps, or three including an honor.

♠ 53　　♥ K953　　♦ 9762　　♣ KQ4

This is a weak hand, but it does have trump support and 9 points, so the response is 2 Hearts. Now the bidding reverts to the opener.

Opener's Next Bid

Your rebid is just a matter of adding your points to the points your partner has shown. If you see no chance for game you pass. If you see game you bid it.

On this hand you know your partner has at least 6 points, your 20 + his 6 = 26. You bid 4 Hearts. This rebid shows 19, 20 or 21 points.

With a Weak Opening

But suppose your hand had been weaker and you didn't have the Ace and King of Spades.

♠ 9864　　♥ AQ762　　♦ 8　　♣ AJ9

The opening bid is still 1 Heart, but when your partner responds 2 Hearts, you see there is no game. Your 13 + his maximum of 10 = 23 so you pass. You don't increase the contract when there's no hope for game.

A Strong Response

However, if your partner had a better hand

♠ 53   ♥ K953   ♦ A972   ♣ KQ4

he would *jump* the bidding to 3 Hearts, showing a minimum of 13. Adding that to yours, you would have 26, so you carry on to 4 Hearts.

Partner's hand is only an Ace better, but it's enough to change his bid. We make *different bids with different hands.*

Flash Card

Opening a Major		
1 ♠ or 1 ♥ shows 13-21 points five trumps 2½ quick tricks	☐	Bid 2 with 6-10 and three trumps Bid 3 with 13-15 and four trumps, *forcing* to game

Playing a Suit Contract

The opening lead against a suit contract is different from the lead against No Trump. You don't lead a suit because it's long but because you might get tricks in it quickly. Usually you'll get tricks only with Aces or Kings or Queens, because the declarer will be trumping when smaller cards are set up.

Choosing the right suit to lead is a problem, but choosing the right card in the suit is routine.

Which Card to Lead

With a singleton you just play it.

With two cards in a suit, lead the higher:

9̲2   J̲3   A̲K

With three cards, lead the top of a sequence in honors, lead low from a single honor, or lead the top of three small cards:

K̲QJ   Q̲J9   K7̲2   105̲3   9̲64

Exception: Lead the King from AK̲5

Avoid leading an Ace because everyone will put little cards on it. Aces are meant to capture Kings and Queens. But if your partner bid a suit, lead it, and if you have the Ace in his suit, lead the Ace.

With four cards or more, lead the top of a sequence or lead fourth best:

K̲Q102   Q763̲2   976̲2

Avoid leading from two honors that don't touch (called a tenace) like KJ3 or Q104, because it will usually cost you a trick.

Which Suit to Lead

The suit you choose to lead is one of the fascinating mysteries of bridge.

If your partner bid a suit, lead it, following the above guideposts.

If you have an attractive card combination, like AK4 or KQJ, lead that suit. You might decide to lead a suit because the opponents bid all the others. Sometimes you have to go from one side of your hand to the other, eliminating the most undesirable of all the undesirables to decide which to lead.

It has been said if you could always make the right opening lead you would win more than anyone ever has in the history of bridge.

Declarer's Play

As soon as declarer obtains the lead, he usually pulls all the opponent's trumps, counting carefully, and then stops and saves his other trumps for ruffing. A good declarer is a pig; he wants to be the only person who can win tricks by trumping.

Then declarer, just as in No Trump contracts, sets up his next best suit and runs it.

II. Major Suit Drill

Opening 1♥ or 1♠ and Responses

1. What is your point count and opening bid?

♠7	♠QJ1076	♠K43	♠K1076	♠KQ103
♥AKQ765	♥AKJ64	♥AQJ	♥A72	♥KQ943
♦K43	♦43	♦QJ543	♦A53	♦AK53
♣KJ3	♣7	♣K2	♣J43	♣---

_____ _____ _____ _____

2. Your partner opened 1♥. What's your response?

♠72	♠72	♠72
♥Q7653	♥Q874	♥Q765
♦986	♦A75	♦AK3
♣972	♣J763	♣K752

_____ _____ _____

3. You   Partner
     1♠   ☐   2♠

What's your rebid?

♠AKQ764	♠AKQ72	♠AQJ72
♥3	♥97	♥KQJ97
♦K72	♦K75	♦5
♣KQ4	♣974	♣K9

_____ _____ _____

5. Bidding a Major

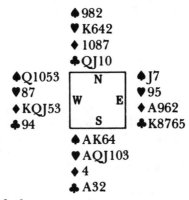

```
              ♠982
              ♥K642
              ♦1087
              ♣QJ10
   ♠Q1053    ┌──────┐   ♠J7
   ♥87       │   N  │    ♥95
   ♦KQJ53    │W    E│    ♦A962
   ♣94       │   S  │    ♣K8765
             └──────┘
              ♠AK64
              ♥AQJ103
              ♦4
              ♣A32
```

South deals
The bidding:

SOUTH	WEST	NORTH	EAST
1 Heart	Pass	2 Hearts	Pass
4 Hearts	Pass	Pass	Pass

South opened 1 Heart. When his partner showed Heart support and six points, he added his 20 and leaped to game.

West had a good lead, the King of Diamonds, the top of a sequence in honors, so he played it and won the trick. Hopefully, he continued with the Queen of Diamonds. Alas, declarer trumped that with his smallest Heart and won the trick.

Declarer counted his tricks and planned his play. He had five Heart tricks, two Spade tricks, two Club tricks, and expected to trump one Spade in dummy. That made 10, just what he bid.

South led the Ace of Hearts and continued with the Queen. Everyone followed to both tricks. Nine Hearts had been played including the trump at trick two. He had four. That made 13 and there were no more out.

Now declarer moved to the side suit that promised the most tricks, Spades.

He cashed the Ace of Spades and then the King. Next he played a little Spade, giving up a trick. West won and continued with the Jack of Diamonds. Declarer ruffed and led another Spade so he could trump in dummy. He led the Queen of Clubs.

This was the Club story.

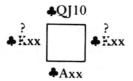

"Who had the King of Clubs?" East played low (second hand low) at a normal tempo not to appear nervous. He didn't want declarer to suspect he had the King of Clubs. But South realized that if East had the King of Clubs he could trap it and if West had the King of Clubs West would eventually get it. South had nothing to lose by playing low . . . and the Queen won the trick.

South had just executed a "finesse", a great way to create tricks in bridge.

Now declarer continued with the Jack of Clubs. Again East played a low card smoothly. He hoped the declarer had only the Ace of Clubs left and had to play it.

Declarer played low again and won. Next he took his Ace of Clubs and had a trump for the last trick, making one over his contract.

The Scoring

Spades and Hearts are "major" suits and count 30 a trick. It takes four to make a game. North-South scored a game below the line and an overtrick above the line. They got 100 for holding four honors in the trump suit in one hand.

We	They
100	
30	
120	

Tips:

The dummy does not put his cards down until after the opening lead has been made.

Always finesse for a King. Half the time it will be dealt to your right-hand opponent and half the time to your left-hand opponent. If you always finesse, you'll win half the time. In finessing lead *toward* the big card. In this case the big card was the Ace of Clubs. Declarer led Clubs from dummy *toward* the Ace.

6. The Responder Jumps

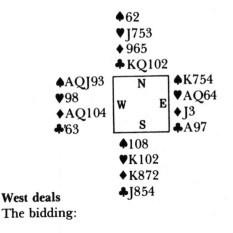

```
                ♠62
                ♥J753
                ♦965
                ♣KQ102
   ♠AQJ93    ┌──────────┐    ♠K754
   ♥98       │    N     │    ♥AQ64
   ♦AQ104    │ W      E │    ♦J3
   ♣63       │    S     │    ♣A97
             └──────────┘
                ♠108
                ♥K102
                ♦K872
                ♣J854
```

West deals
The bidding:

WEST	NORTH	EAST	SOUTH
1 Spade	Pass	3 Spades	Pass
4 Spades	Pass	Pass	Pass

West counted 13 high-card points and added two for his Club and Heart doubletons. He opened his five-card major.

East gave a jump raise showing 13 to 15 and trump support. He had 13 highs and got one for his doubleton; he couldn't count the Jack of Diamonds because it wasn't protected.

West went to 4 Spades and became declarer.

North had a safe lead, the King of Clubs. He didn't have a perfect sequence, but it was the next best thing, two touching honors, a skip, and the next ranking card.

Declarer won with dummy's Ace and then stopped to count his tricks, five Spades, three Diamonds, one Heart and one Club = 10. Then he had a chance for two overtricks if he could trap the King of Diamonds and the King of Hearts.

First he pulled the opponents' trumps, playing the Ace and then the King. Then he attacked his next best suit, Diamonds.

He led the Jack of Diamonds. South played low, the declarer laid down the 4 of Diamonds, and North followed with the 5. His finesse worked! He continued with the 3 of Diamonds and played his 10, which won the trick. Now he laid down the Ace of Diamonds, discarding a Club from dummy and was disappointed that the King didn't fall.

Declarer switched to Hearts to try another finesse. He led the 9 and put in the Queen, but South captured it with the King.

South returned his partner's opening Club lead with the Jack. It won. He led the King of Diamonds, but declarer ruffed in dummy, took his Ace of Hearts and then he claimed the rest of the tricks, because his hand was all trumps. He made an overtrick.

Now each side had a game. The next side to win a game would get the rubber bonus. The score now was:

We	They
100	
30	30
120	
	120

7. Another Jump Response

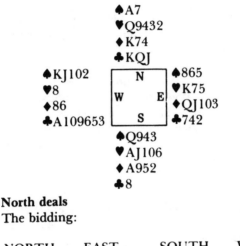

```
                    ♠ A7
                    ♥ Q9432
                    ♦ K74
                    ♣ KQJ
      ♠ KJ102         N        ♠ 865
      ♥ 8                      ♥ K75
      ♦ 86        W     E      ♦ QJ103
      ♣ A109653      S         ♣ 742
                    ♠ Q943
                    ♥ AJ106
                    ♦ A952
                    ♣ 8
```

North deals

The bidding:

NORTH	EAST	SOUTH	WEST
1 Heart	Pass	3 Hearts	Pass
4 Hearts	Pass	Pass	Pass

North counted 15 highs plus 1 distributional point and opened his five-card major, 1 Heart. South, with a full opening hand and trump support, was delighted to give a double raise and North bid a game.

East selected the Queen of Diamonds for the opening lead. North counted his tricks and found he had a loser in each suit. Maybe he could pick up the trump King with a finesse. He let the Diamond ride around to his King to be ready for the trump play.

Declarer played the Queen of Hearts, East played low and the Queen won. Now he led a small Heart, again East laid down a small one, and dummy's 10 won.

Declarer counted the trumps and found there was just one out so he played the Ace to pick up the King.

Now he led a Club and West took the Ace and re-turned a Diamond to his partner. Dummy's Ace won.

Declarer came to his hand with the Ace of Spades and then cashed the King and Queen of Clubs, dis-carding two Diamonds from dummy.

He led a Diamond and trumped it in dummy. He gave up a Spade trick and had the last two tricks with his good trumps. He made five and won a 500 rubber. The score stands:

	We	They
	500	
	30	
	100	
	30	30
	120	
		120
	120	
Total:	900	150

8. A Single Raise

```
                ♠9753
                ♥A53
                ♦Q864
                ♣103
      ♠64          N          ♠AQJ
      ♥J864                   ♥KQ972
      ♦95      W       E      ♦AK32
      ♣A8764       S          ♣2
                ♠K1082
                ♥10
                ♦J107
                ♣KQJ95
```

East deals
The bidding:

EAST	SOUTH	WEST	NORTH
1 Heart	Pass	2 Hearts	Pass
4 Hearts	Pass	Pass	Pass

East was elated to find 21 points in his hand and opened 1 Heart. West barely had a raise but it was enough and East leaped to game.

South led the King of Clubs and declarer hopped up with dummy's Ace.

He counted his tricks: four Hearts, two Spades, two Diamonds, one Club. That was nine and if he could trump one Diamond in dummy, he'd have his game.

He led a low Heart, North played low, and declarer won the Queen. He continued with the King of Hearts. North took it with his Ace and returned a Club to his partner but Declarer stepped out with a trump and won the trick. Then he led to the Jack of Hearts to pull the lone outstanding trump.

He came off dummy with a little Spade inserting the Jack. The finesse lost to the King. South pressed on with another Club which declarer ruffed with the last trump in his hand.

He cashed the Ace and Queen of Spades, took the Ace and King of Diamonds, trumped a Diamond in dummy and gave up the last trick to South's high Club. He squeaked through with his game.

It's a new rubber; you can score this one by yourself.

III. BIDDING ONE DIAMOND OR ONE CLUB

The first thing you ask yourself when you arrange your cards at bridge is, "Can I bid 1 No Trump?" The next is, "Can I bid 1 Spade or 1 Heart?" Take this hand:

♠AKxx ♥AJxx ♦x ♣KQxx

You have 17 high-card points but you can't bid 1 No Trump because you have uneven distribution. All those beautiful points and you can't bid 1 Spade or 1 Heart because you need five cards in a major. Even a weaker hand with only 13 points is biddable so what are you going to say? Bid 1 Club.

The Convenient Minor

Although we seldom play a contract in Diamonds or Clubs, we often bid them to show an opening hand and to begin a search for a game somewhere else. You bid whichever is longer. You only need three cards in the suit.

Diamonds and Clubs are called the minor suits because they only count 20 points a trick. You have to bid five to get a game; that's promising to take eleven tricks which is very hard to do. It takes 29 points, which you seldom get. You would always rather play the less expensive contracts of 3 No Trump, 4 Spades, or 4 Hearts.

The suits have rank. Clubs are the lowest, followed by Diamonds, Hearts, and Spades. That makes Spades a very special suit because it tops any other in the bidding. Since you opened 1 Club your partner can bid any suit at the 1 level, keeping the bidding low while you search for the best contract.

Responding to a Minor

Once you have opened the bidding, your partner will respond with as few as six points. He will bid his longest suit first. A six-card suit takes precedence over a five-card suit. If he has neither *he can bid any four-card suit as long as he can bid it at the 1-level.* If he has more than one four-card suit he bids the *lowest ranking* first.

Thus, with four Hearts and four Spades he responds a Heart because Hearts rank lower than Spades. If he has four Diamonds and four Hearts he bids a Diamond because Diamonds rank lower than Hearts. This gives each of the suits a chance to surface as the trump suit.

Let's go back to your opening bid of 1 Club. Your partner has:

♠Qxxx   ♥Kxx   ♦10x   ♣Jxxx

Should he raise Clubs? No, he should try to find a better spot. He bids 1 Spade. That bid tells you he has at least four cards in the Spade suit and 6 or more points.

See if you can find the correct response on these hands after an opening of 1 Club:

1. ♠KJxxx   ♥QJxx   ♦ Ax   ♣xx
2. ♠KJxx   ♥QJxx   ♦ xx   ♣xxx
3. ♠KJxx   ♥xxx   ♦QJxxx ♣x

III. BIDDING ONE DIAMOND
OR ONE CLUB

The first thing you ask yourself when you arrange your cards at bridge is, "Can I bid 1 No Trump?" The next is, "Can I bid 1 Spade or 1 Heart?" Take this hand:

♠AKxx   ♥AJxx   ♦x   ♣KQxx

You have 17 high-card points but you can't bid 1 No Trump because you have uneven distribution. All those beautiful points and you can't bid 1 Spade or 1 Heart because you need five cards in a major. Even a weaker hand with only 13 points is biddable so what are you going to say? Bid 1 Club.

The Convenient Minor

Although we seldom play a contract in Diamonds or Clubs, we often bid them to show an opening hand and to begin a search for a game somewhere else. You bid whichever is longer. You only need three cards in the suit.

Diamonds and Clubs are called the minor suits because they only count 20 points a trick. You have to bid five to get a game; that's promising to take eleven tricks which is very hard to do. It takes 29 points, which you seldom get. You would always rather play the less expensive contracts of 3 No Trump, 4 Spades, or 4 Hearts.

In the first hand he has seven points and he would pass. Even if the opener is on the top of his bid, there's no chance for a game (15 + 7 = only 22).

On the second hand he has 15. No matter how weak the opening bid was he sees game (13 + 15 = 28) and be bids it, 4 Spades.

Without that Fit

Let's examine another alternative. Let's change your opening hand to:

♠AKxx   ♥xxx   ♦x   ♣KQxxx

You still open a Club, but your partner responds a Heart. Now what? You can't raise Hearts because you don't have four cards in the suit. You can now bid any four-card suit as long as you can name it at the 1 level. Bid 1 Spade.

In this system it is possible for the bidding to go:

| 1 Club | Pass | 1 Diamond | Pass |
| 1 Heart | Pass | 1 Spade | Pass |

Your side has made four bids, you have exchanged lots of information, and you're still at the 1 level.

This is the way we find a four-four fit in a trump suit, four in your hand and four in your partner's, making the eight we need.

It is called up-the-line bidding and it has swept the bridge world.

On the first hand, it's 1 Spade, the longest suit first. On the next hand, with two four-card suits, it's the lower ranking first, 1 Heart. On the third the bid is 1 Diamond, the longest first.

Rebid by the Opener

When your partner responds to your opening bid with a new suit, he forces you to bid again. If you have four cards in the suit your partner named, let him know a trump suit has been found by raising him, and tell him how many points you have. You give a single raise with 13 to 15 points, a single jump with 16-18, and jump to game with 19 to 21 points. Let's look at three examples:

1. ♠AKxx   ♥AJxx   ♦x   ♣KQxx
2. ♠AKxx   ♥xxxx   ♦x   ♣KQxx
3. ♠AKJx   ♥Qxxx   ♦x   ♣KQxx

On each of these hands you'd open 1 Club. Your partner bids 1 Spade. What's your rebid?

On the first hand you leap to game, 4 Spades. On the second you would only raise to 2 Spades. On the third you give a jump raise. The level of your raise shows the difference in the point count.

Responder's Second Bid

Let's assume the opener gave a single raise. The bidding reverts to the responder and he places the final contract. He adds his points to his partner's. With a weak hand of 6-10 points he'll pass; with a good hand of 13-15 he'll go to game. Here are two examples.

1. ♠Qxxx   ♥Kxx   ♦xx   ♣Jxxx
2. ♠Qxxx   ♥Kxx   ♦Ax   ♣AJxx

Tip

Responding to a minor when you hold two five-card suits, bid the higher ranking first. Holding ♠A7654 ♥KQ 765 ♦J2 ♣9, respond 1 Spade. If partner doesn't raise Spades, next time bid Hearts.

Flash Card

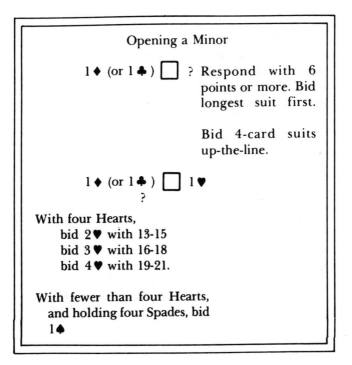

Opening a Minor

1 ♦ (or 1 ♣) ☐ ? Respond with 6 points or more. Bid longest suit first.

Bid 4-card suits up-the-line.

1 ♦ (or 1 ♣) ☐ 1 ♥
?

With four Hearts,
    bid 2 ♥ with 13-15
    bid 3 ♥ with 16-18
    bid 4 ♥ with 19-21.

With fewer than four Hearts,
    and holding four Spades, bid
    1 ♠

III. Opening 1♦ or 1♣ Drill

1. What's your point count and opening bid?

♠AK72	♠J875	♠K762	♠K765
♥QJ87	♥K975	♥K82	♥AK42
♦A43	♦AK	♦K72	♦AK
♣82	♣K82	♣AQJ	♣Q65

——————— ——————— ——————— ———————

2. Your partner opened 1♣. What's your point count and response?

♠KJ32	♠AKJ7	♠A765	♠AK
♥Q752	♥K53	♥K3	♥J654
♦87	♦A3	♦K8765	♦74
♣876	♣J754	♣J2	♣KJ765

——————— ——————— ——————— ———————

3. You   Partner
    1♣   ☐   1♥

What's your rebid?

♠KJ72	♠KQ72	♠J762	♠J65
♥AK65	♥J832	♥AK5	♥AQ
♦K3	♦K4	♦72	♦32
♣AJ8	♣AJ3	♣AQ5	♣AQ8765

——————— ——————— ——————— ———————

4. The bidding has gone:

	Partner	You
	1♣	1♥
What do you say with:	1♠	?

♠Q765	♠KQ76	♠76	♠73
♥AQ65	♥KQJ5	♥A763	♥A7654
♦765	♦J53	♦86	♦KQJ5
♣54	♣52	♣QJ654	♣K3

——————— ——————— ——————— ———————

9. Opening a Minor

```
              ♠ J852
              ♥ J1064
              ♦ AK
              ♣ AJ7
  ♠ AK74      ┌─────────┐      ♠ Q93
  ♥ 92        │    N    │      ♥ Q75
  ♦ J10942    │ W     E │      ♦ Q76
  ♣ 93        │    S    │      ♣ 10642
              └─────────┘
              ♠ 106
              ♥ AK83
              ♦ 853
              ♣ KQ85
```

North deals
The bidding:

NORTH	EAST	SOUTH	WEST
1 Club	Pass	1 Heart	Pass
2 Hearts	Pass	4 Hearts	Pass
Pass	Pass		

North counted his cards at 15 points and opened his better minor, "1 Club." South showed his four-card major, "1 Heart." On his rebid North confirmed the trump suit, but said he had a minimum opener. With 13 points South jumped to game. An opening hand facing an opening hand usually produces game.

South named Hearts first so he was the declarer and that gave West the opening lead. He had two sequences in honors. (Two is a sequence against a suit contract.) But the Ace and King of Spades were going to take tricks quicker than the Jack and 10 of Diamonds, so he led the King of Spades. When it was East's turn to play, he wanted to tell his partner to keep leading Spades because he had a Spade trick, too. He played the 9.

Signalling High-Low

Defending against a declarer is difficult because East and West can't see each other's cards. Defenders use their inconsequential cards to send messages to each other. When a player follows with a high card and then a low card, playing out-of-order, it's a signal requesting his partner to keep leading that suit. It's called the high-low signal.

In starting a high-low signal, try to begin with a 6 or higher, because a 6 or above is considered a "come-on" card.

Let's go back to West's lead of the King and East's play of the 9. That 9 was a beckoning card so West did what his partner asked and continued the suit, playing the Ace of Spades. Now East played the 3 of Spades, completing the high-low signal. West led a low Spade to East's Queen, but declarer jumped in with a trump and won the trick.

Finessing for a Queen

South counted his tricks and outlined his play. He had taken a trump trick and had the Ace and King of Hearts; the Ace, King, Queen, Jack of Clubs were four more; the Ace and King of Diamonds were two and he could trump a Diamond in dummy. That made ten tricks. The only loser he had was the Jack of Hearts which could be won by the Queen.

Where was the Queen of Hearts?

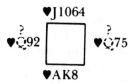

If East had the Queen, declarer could trap it by leading the Jack from dummy. If East covered, South would cover; if East played low, South would play low.

If West had it, declarer would have to lose it, because West would play after the declarer. There was a 50 per cent chance that East had it, so declarer played for that chance. There is a rhyme that tells you when to finesse for a queen:

> "Eight ever,
> Nine never."

With only eight cards in the suit and a Queen missing, finesse; with nine cards in the suit, just lay down the Ace and the King and hope the Queen falls.

In finessing, we lead *toward* our big card, so South had to get to dummy to lead Hearts. He played a small Diamond to the King and now dummy was on lead. He pulled out the Jack of Hearts, East played low, South played low . . . West played low. The Jack won!

Now he cashed the Ace and King of Hearts and the Queen fell. The opponents were out of trumps.

Next declarer played his most promising side suit, Clubs. He led a little Club to the Ace, took the Jack, and now crossed over to his King and Queen. He played a Diamond to the Ace and played the last trump. He took eleven tricks, one more than he bid.

10. Showing a Minimum

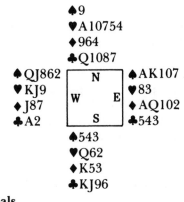

```
              ♠9
              ♥A10754
              ♦964
              ♣Q1087
♠QJ862    ┌─────────┐   ♠AK107
♥KJ9      │    N    │   ♥83
♦J87      │ W     E │   ♦AQ102
♣A2       │    S    │   ♣543
          └─────────┘
              ♠543
              ♥Q62
              ♦K53
              ♣KJ96
```

East deals
The bidding:

EAST	SOUTH	WEST	NORTH
1 Diamond	Pass	1 Spade	Pass
2 Spades	Pass	4 Spades	Pass
Pass	Pass		

East had 13 highs and one distributional point and opened his stronger minor, 1 Diamond. West showed his longest suit, "1 Spade." East agreed on the trump choice and showed a minimum opener by raising to 2 Spades. It was back to West who added his 12 + 1 to his partner's and skipped to 4 Spades.

North searched for a lead. He didn't want to lead the two suits bid by the opponents but he didn't like his Heart or Club holdings. Finally, he chose the Club 7.

Declarer counted five Spade tricks, three or four Diamonds, one Club, and maybe a Heart. Nine tricks and two possible. If he could make a successful finesse in either of the red suits he'd make his contract.

He took the Club Ace, led to the Ace of Spades, then played to the Jack. There was still a trump out so he played the Queen and gathered it in.

It was time to test the Diamond suit and West brought out the Jack. North followed low, the dummy low, and South came up with the King. That finesse failed. Now South switched to the Club 6 and North won the 10; he continued the Queen of Clubs. Declarer trumped.

Declarer led to the Ace of Diamonds, picked up the Queen, and then the 10, on the last discarding a Heart. Here's the Heart story:

♥A10754

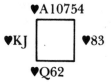

♥KJ   ♥83

♥Q62

He led the 8 of Hearts, South played low, and declarer finessed with the Jack. It forced the Ace. This finesse worked. Declarer trumped the Club return and played the King of Hearts. He lost one trick in each of the side suits, making four Spades exactly.

11. Opener Rebids a 4-Card Major

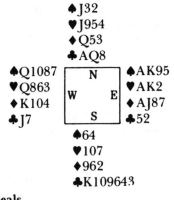

```
                    ♠J32
                    ♥J954
                    ♦Q53
                    ♣AQ8
      ♠Q1087      ┌──────────┐    ♠AK95
      ♥Q863       │    N     │    ♥AK2
      ♦K104       │ W     E  │    ♦AJ87
      ♣J7         │    S     │    ♣52
                  └──────────┘
                    ♠64
                    ♥107
                    ♦962
                    ♣K109643
```

South deals

The bidding:

SOUTH	WEST	NORTH	EAST
Pass	Pass	Pass	1 Diamond
Pass	1 Heart	Pass	1 Spade
Pass	2 Spades	Pass	4 Spades

Three passes to East who had 19 highs + 1 distributional point and opened 1 Diamond. West responded a Heart and East bid a Spade. West showed the trump fit and a minimum response with 2 Spades. East climbed to game.

South elected to open the only unbid suit and led his fourth best, the 6 of Clubs. North went up with the Ace and returned the Queen which won. Now North faced the problem of a lead and switched to the 4 of Hearts. South played the 10 and dummy's Queen won.

Declarer counted four Spades, three Hearts and

three diamonds, making 10. He'd get another if he could guess who had the Queen of Diamonds.

He played a low Spade to the King, then a low one back to the Queen, now another to the Ace and all the trumps were in. He took the Ace and King of Hearts.

It was time to take the Diamond guess. He could finesse either way because he held the Jack and the 10.

♦K104 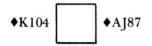 ♦AJ87

He played a low one to the King and led the 10. North played low and declarer let it ride to victory. Next, a low Diamond and the Queen came tumbling down; declarer took the Ace. Now the Jack of Diamonds was high and East had a high trump. He took eleven tricks. If declarer had guessed the Diamond wrong he would still have made his contract, but he gave himself a chance for an overtrick by trying the finesse.

12. Taking Responder to Game

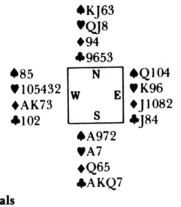

West deals
The bidding:

WEST	NORTH	EAST	SOUTH
Pass	Pass	Pass	1 Club
Pass	1 Spade	Pass	4 Spades
Pass	Pass	Pass	

With 19 highs, South was too strong to bid a No Trump so he opened 1 Club. North had a weak hand, 7 + 1, but eked out a response of 1 Spade. South leaped to game.

East started the activity with the Diamond Jack, low from dummy, and West invited with the 7. When the Jack held, East continued the 10 — covered by the Queen — and West took his King. West tried the Diamond Ace but declarer ruffed.

Counting his winners, declarer saw he could lose to the Queen of Spades and the King of Hearts. If he could win either finesse, he'd be safe.

♠KJ63

♠A972

He played a low Spade to the Ace and returned a Spade — trying the Jack — but it lost to the Queen.

Seeing no good alternative, East continued the trump and declarer took the King. Declarer needed to make the Heart play from his hand.

♥QJ8

♥A7

He laid down the Queen of Hearts, East covered, hoping his partner had the Jack, and dummy's Ace won. Now declarer took the Jack of Hearts and ran the Clubs, the Ace, the King, the Queen — and the little Club was good. The last trick went to dummy's trump. Declarer was able to make four because one of his finesses won. The finesse is the greatest way to *create* tricks in bridge.

Tips:

When defending you also signal high-low when you can take the third round by trumping:

A<u>K</u>72   ☐   <u>9</u>6

just as you do when you want to take the third trick with a Queen

A<u>K</u>72   ☐   Q<u>9</u>6

Sometimes you don't get picturesque cards for signalling. You just do the best you can. With the Q32 East would play the 3. Following to partner's lead with 2's, 3's, 4's, or 5's usually disclaims any interest in the continuation of that suit. You'll just have to hope your partner looks around and finds the 2 missing.

When you are discarding you can also flash the high-low signal to ask your partner to lead a suit. Declarer is playing a Heart contract and leading trumps. You don't have any. You'd like a Diamond lead from partner.

♦AK762

Discard the 7 and then the 2. That says, "Please lead Diamonds!"

IV. THE OVERCALL

You're ready on this hand:

♠AKQ72   ♥8   ♦KQ4   ♣9875

Fourteen high-card points and a five-card major. It's 1 Spade. You're learning to bid! But before it is your turn to bid the dealer, your right-hand opponent, calls, "1 Heart." Now what do you do?

You *overcall* 1 Spade. You have just said to your partner, "I have a *good* suit with at least five cards in it and approximately an opening bid."

You promise an opening bid but sometimes you make an overcall at the one level with as few as 10 points to tell your partner what suit you'd like led.

An overcall of one in a suit shows 10 to 15 points and two of the three top honors in the suit.

When you overcall at the two level you need an opening hand so that bid shows 13 to 15 points. (What to do with stronger hands will be studied in Chapter VII.)

When you overcall you bid your suit at the lowest level. You were lucky to have the Spade suit and be able to come in with a one bid. Suppose your black suits were reversed and your long suit had been Clubs. Hearts outrank Clubs so you would have to bid 2 Clubs.

Responding to an Overcall

Let's go back to your overcall of 1 Spade. How does your partner respond? He treats it like an opening bid. With three cards in your suit and 6 to 10 points he will give you a single raise and say, "2 Spades." With support in your suit and 11, 12 or 13 points he will jump the bidding and say, "3 Spades."

The bidding is similar to responses to an opening bid with two exceptions. Notice the jump raise of an overcall is made on a slightly weaker holding than the jump raise of an opening bid and it is *not forcing* to game.

When you make a weak overcall and your partner gives a jump raise you do not carry on to game. You pass. When the overcall is made on full values, however, you can go on to game.

If your hand had been:

♠AKQ72   ♥8   ♦854   ♣9875

you would still overcall 1 Spade, but if your partner gave you a jump raise you would pass because you overcalled without full values.

At the Two Level

The overcall at the two level is more dangerous. The opponents bid 1 Heart and you have:

♠965   ♥82   ♦AKQ72   ♣975

You pass. Your hand has only 10 points and isn't good

enough for 2 Diamonds. If your opponent had opened 1 Club you could have said 1 Diamond.

♠xxx   ♥Kx   ♦KJ742   ♣AJx

Again your opponent opened 1 Heart. You have an opening hand but your suit is too weak to overcall 2 Diamonds. You could run into an unfortunate trump break. Pass. With another top honor — ♦KQJ74 or ♦AQJ74 — you'd be happy to overcall 2 Diamonds.

The No Trump Overcall

The 1 No Trump overcall is identical to an opening 1 No Trump with the restriction that the adversary's suit must be safely stopped.

1♠   ♠KJ8   ♥AK4   ♦AQJ6   ♣1087

Bid 1 No Trump. If partner is weak you're prepared to play it. If he raises you want to go to game.

How to Respond When There's an Overcall

Now let's go back to the opening bid of 1 Heart. What happens to the opener's partner when you overcalled:

He responds, naturally. With three of his partner's suit and 6 to 10 points he raises one; with four-card support and 13 to 15 points he jumps to 3 Hearts. The jump forces the opener to go to 4 Hearts.

Overcalling Strategy

Overcalling is an important part of a winning player's strategy. First, you have told your partner what to lead. That's very important because finding the best opening lead is the most difficult play in bridge. Second, you might win the auction and get a part score or a game. Third, you have complicated the bidding for the opponents. You have made it more difficult for them to find their suit and describe their point count.

A lot of bidding scares some people out of the auction. Don't be afraid to bid your points. Listen to your partner and add your hand to his. Often the points are so evenly divided between the two sides that no one can make a game. There are hands that will make 2 Hearts for one side and 2 Spades for the other. In that event, if you have Hearts, you want to win the contract at 2 Hearts and some timid opponents might let you. However, if they push on to 2 Spades you might prefer to sacrifice at 3 Hearts.

For bidding and making 2 Spades your opponents will score 60 *below* the line where it counts toward a game. If you bid 3 Hearts and go down one they only get 50 and it's *above* the line.

You want to be wise when you overbid and not risk too much. It is foolhardy to go down three, especially if you're doubled. That's 500.

What it Costs To Go Down

When you bid more than you can make you don't get any score (unless you had honors). The opponents chalk up 50 for each trick they set you. If you have a game you're so near winning a rubber you become "vulnerable" and the penalty swells to 100 a trick.

Now if the opponents think they can set you they say "double" and get even richer if you go down.

Not-Vulnerable, Doubled

100 for the 1st, 200 for 2nd and 3rd,
300 for each thereafter

Vulnerable, Doubled

200 for the 1st, 300 each after

If you doubled the opponents when they were vulnerable and set them three tricks you'd get 800 points. That's more than the bonus for winning a rubber.

If you didn't double you'd only get 300; that's about a third as much. You want to double when your opponents climb out on a limb and you know they can't make their contract.

However, if you double and they make their bid they get extra. The trick score below the line is doubled. Two Spades doubled and made is a game 60 x 2 = 120. Above the line there is a premium of 50 for fulfilling a doubled contract, and overtricks are 100 not-vulnerable and 200 vulnerable.

Now you know two ways to make a big score at bridge, to win a rubber and to double and set the opponents.

Flash Card

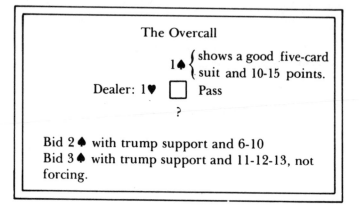

The Overcall

1♠ { shows a good five-card suit and 10-15 points.

Dealer: 1♥ ☐ Pass

?

Bid 2♠ with trump support and 6-10
Bid 3♠ with trump support and 11-12-13, not forcing.

IV. The Overcall Drill

1. Your opponent opened 1♥. It's your turn next. What do you say with:

♠AKQ765	♠98	♠875	♠A74	♠8
♥8	♥AK1094	♥654	♥AQ4	♥96
♦K76	♦AQ76	♦AKQ87	♦KJ76	♦AQJ74
♣865	♣43	♣74	♣K52	♣KQ763

_____   _____   _____   _____

2. The bidding has gone:

1 Diamond   1 Spade   Pass   ?

What do you bid with:

♠A72	♠KJ8	♠KQ72
♥KQ765	♥QJ62	♥875
♦76	♦32	♦654
♣654	♣KQ52	♣542

_____   _____   _____

3. The bidding went:

1 Heart   1 Spade   ?

What do you bid with:

♠K32	♠AJ7	♠8642
♥KQ43	♥J2	♥QJ53
♦8532	♦Q752	♦A75
♣42	♣J872	♣AK

_____   _____   _____

13. Competing for the Contract

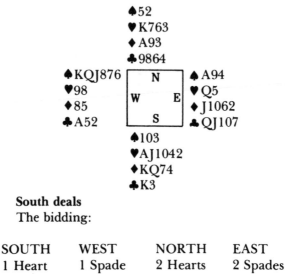

♠52
♥K763
♦A93
♣9864

♠KQJ876
♥98
♦85
♣A52

♠A94
♥Q5
♦J1062
♣QJ107

♠103
♥AJ1042
♦KQ74
♣K3

South deals
The bidding:

SOUTH	WEST	NORTH	EAST
1 Heart	1 Spade	2 Hearts	2 Spades
??			

Will South compete? If South bids 3 Hearts will West try 3 Spades? Practice playing this hand with Hearts as trumps and then with Spades as Trumps.

South Plays 3 Hearts

West led the King of Spades, the top of his sequence in honors, and won the trick, East encouraging with the 9. West continued the Queen which held the trick. Seeing dummy ready to trump Spades West decided to switch — but to what? He didn't want to lead Clubs because if he led the Ace everyone would put little cards on it and he wanted to get something bigger. He didn't want to lead a small Club because declarer might have the singleton King. As the lesser of the two evils, he played a Diamond, the 8, top of a doubleton.

South won the Queen of Diamonds and immediately drew the opponents trumps. He played to the King and then back to the Ace. The Queen fell but he never intended to finesse because he had nine cards in the suit. All the Hearts were in so South turned his attention to his best side suit, Diamonds, cashing the Ace and next the King. He then trumped his last Diamond in dummy.

Declarer led a Club, East played the 10, declarer went up with the King and West jumped on it with his Ace. Now West played a Club to his partner's Jack. East led the Queen of Clubs but the party was over. Declarer trumped it and had another trump left to take the last trick. He made 3 Hearts.

West Plays 3 Spades

If West competed with 3 Spades it would be North's opening lead. He wanted to lead his partner's suit. Which card would describe his holding? The 3, promising an honor or four cards in the suit. Dummy played low and South stepped smartly in with the 10. He believed his partner had the King but if declarer had it declarer would eventually get it anyway. The 10 won.

South cashed the Ace of Hearts and then switched to the King of Diamonds. It won as partner lured him on with the 9. South continued with the Queen and then played a third round of Diamonds. Declarer trumped and took over.

First the declarer pulled the opponents' trumps, playing the King and then the Ace. He had a reason for playing the Ace last. If trumps cleared he wanted to lead Clubs from the dummy to finesse against the King.

♣A52   ♣QJ107

He led the Queen of Clubs and everyone played low. Then he led the Jack, covered by the King, and declarer won the Ace. Now he took the high 10 of Clubs and had all good trumps remaining, taking nine tricks.

If the finesse had failed and North had the King of Clubs, the 3 Spade contract would be set but West wouldn't be sorry he bid it. He would rather lose 50 above the line than 90 below.

Tip:

When we have a sequence in honors we lead the top of it, but when we are following to a trick we play the low card in the sequence. Here the 9 is led, top of nothing.

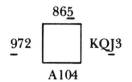

When the Jack forces the Ace partner realizes you may have the King and Queen.

14. Overcalling 1 No Trump

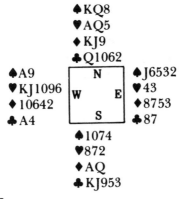

♠ KQ8
♥ AQ5
♦ KJ9
♣ Q1062

♠ A9
♥ KJ1096
♦ 10642
♣ A4

♠ J6532
♥ 43
♦ 8753
♣ 87

♠ 1074
♥ 872
♦ AQ
♣ KJ953

West deals
The bidding:

WEST	NORTH	EAST	SOUTH
1 Heart	1 NT	Pass	3 NT
Pass	Pass	Pass	

With 14 points West began with a Heart, North overcalled a No Trump, East passed, and South bid 3 No Trump.

East opened his partner's suit, the 4 of Hearts, the top of a doubleton. West played the King and declarer snapped it up with the Ace.

North counted his tricks — four Clubs, three Diamonds, two Hearts, and two Spades. But he foresaw that he couldn't get all of those. When West got in with one black Ace, he would drive out declarer's other Heart stopper. When he won the second black Ace, the Hearts would be good.

It was crucial for North to drive out the Club Ace first because that would insure his contract with four tricks in Clubs, three in Diamonds, and two in Hearts.

Declarer played the Queen of Clubs which was taken by West's Ace. West laid down the Jack of Hearts and declarer took the Queen and went back to his specialty, the Clubs. He collected the 10, then dummy's King, Jack, and 9. Next the Ace of Diamonds, the Queen *overtaken* by the King so the Jack could win a trick before the Walls of Jericho came crashing down.

The King of Spades was tried but West took the Ace and his 10 and 9 of Hearts to win the last three tricks. North made his 3 No Trump by the skin of his teeth.

15. Indicating a Lead

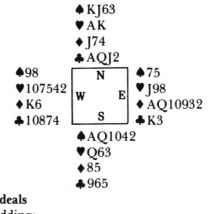

```
                    ♠ KJ63
                    ♥ AK
                    ♦ J74
                    ♣ AQJ2
      ♠ 98          ┌─────────┐        ♠ 75
      ♥ 107542      │    N    │        ♥ J98
      ♦ K6          │ W     E │        ♦ AQ10932
      ♣ 10874       │    S    │        ♣ K3
                    └─────────┘
                    ♠ AQ1042
                    ♥ Q63
                    ♦ 85
                    ♣ 965
```

North deals
The bidding:

NORTH	EAST	SOUTH	WEST
1 Club	1 Diamond	1 Spade	Pass
4 Spades	Pass	Pass	Pass

North's hand was too big for an opening No Trump so he began with 1 Club. East overcalled his long suit, "1 Diamond". South came in with 1 Spade and the opener, with 20 points, went to game.

West led the top of his Diamond doubleton, the King. East invited a continuation with the 9. Now West played the 6 and East took the Ace. He returned the Queen.

Since declarer had plenty of high trumps he went in with the big 10 and West couldn't over-ruff. Now South pulled the opponents' trumps, leading to the King and then back the Ace.

He moved to Clubs and let the Jack ride but East's King topped it. East chose a safe Heart exit and declarer took the Ace and then the King of Hearts. Now South played the Ace and Queen of Clubs, ruffed a Club in his hand, and still had a winning trump and the high Queen of Hearts. He made four.

The danger in the hand was to ruff Diamonds too low. It's an old bridge adage, "Don't send out a boy (a little trump) to do a big man's work." Declarer had a wealth of big ones and could afford the 10 spot.

16. Bidding Game After an Overcall

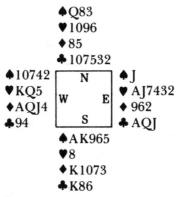

East deals
The bidding:

EAST	SOUTH	WEST	NORTH
1 Heart	1 Spade	3 Hearts	Pass
4 Hearts	Pass	Pass	Pass

East opened a Heart on his minimum hand and South came in with 1 Spade. West jumped to 3 Hearts. He didn't have four trumps but he had two big honors for solace. East carried on to game.

South headed off with the King of Spades and won the trick as his partner invited with the 8. The Ace of Spades came out but declarer romped on it with a tiny Heart.

East counted six trump tricks and two Diamonds and two Clubs. He felt sure he knew where the two missing Kings were — in the overcaller's hand — but he decided to finesse for both.

Declarer played the King of Hearts, the Queen of

Hearts, and then led a low one to the Ace to gather in all the trumps.

Then he led a Diamond and brought out the Jack to win the finesse. He played a Club back and tried the Jack but lost to the King. South chose to continue Clubs and declarer collected the Queen. Next he tried a low Diamond to the Queen which captured the trick and he led the Diamond Ace. Declarer held two good trumps and the Ace of Clubs. That made eleven tricks.

East crossed from one hand to the other as he finessed Clubs and Diamonds. Some players would go down on this simple hand trying to trump all those Spades. The declarer's trumps were always good. The business at hand was to set up the Diamond and Club honors.

V. BIDDING A SLAM

One of the most exciting events that happens at the bridge table is the bidding and making of a slam. To bid *six* — contracting to take all the tricks but one — is a *"small slam"* and to bid *seven* — contracting to take all the tricks — is a *"grand slam."*

Bridge players like fishermen will talk for weeks about the one they brought in or the one that got away. You get a big bonus on your score when you land one. Frequently a slam is the difference between winning and losing in an evening of bridge.

Slam Requirements

It takes 33 points to make a little slam. You can remember that because 3 + 3 = 6 and a little slam is six tricks over your book. It takes 37 points to make a grand slam. Your memory cue is "7 makes seven", and a grand slam is seven tricks over your book.

A Slam in No Trump

You just picked up one of your favorite holdings:

♠K94   ♥A72   ♦Q93   ♣AKJ4

and you're ready to open one No Trump. Your partner was the dealer so it's his turn to bid first. He calls, "One

No Trump". Wow! He has to have 16 points for that bid so you start adding, his 16 + your 17 = 33. That's a small slam. When it's your turn to bid you say, "Six No Trump". You have the point count to bring in 12 tricks.

You will seldom get a hand that is much stronger, but suppose you had four more points.

♠AK9　　♥A72　　◆Q93　　♣AKJ4

Now you have 21 points, his 16 + your 21 = 37. Your bid is "7 No Trump".

A Slam in a Suit

No Trump slam bidding is simple arithmetic. You just add your points to your partner's. Bidding a slam in a suit is more complicated. With short-suit points — voids, singletons and doubletons — there are more than 40 points in the deck. Suppose you opened 1 Spade, your partner jumped to 3 Spades, and your hand was:

♠AKJ72　　♥4　　◆AQ9　　♣K532

When you add your 19 points to your partner's 13 to 15 you get between 32 and 34 points. You're in the small slam zone.

It's crucial in making a slam try in a suit to determine if the opponents have two Aces which they can cash quickly and set you. On this hand you want to know if your partner has one of the two missing Aces.

Blackwood for Aces

There's a way to ask your partner how many Aces

he has. It is called "Blackwood" because it was originated by Easley Blackwood. It is to jump to 4 No Trump, an artificial "asking" bid. It has nothing to do with wanting to play No Trump. It asks your partner, "How many Aces do you have?" The answers are up-the-line by the rank of the suits:

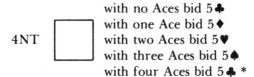

4NT

with no Aces bid 5♣
with one Ace bid 5♦
with two Aces bid 5♥
with three Aces bid 5♠
with four Aces bid 5♣ *

Let's go back to your Spade hand. You ask your partner how many Aces he has by bidding 4 No Trump. Suppose your partner answered 5 Diamonds showing one Ace, you would bid 6 Spades.

Now assume your partner didn't have any Aces at all and he answered 5 Clubs. You would sign-off with 5 Spades and your partner would pass. The person who bid 4 No Trump is the captain and decides how high to go. When he throws in the sponge the partner always passes.

Blackwood for Kings

Take that same hand of yours and make it stronger:

♠AKJ72   ♥4   ♦AKQ   ♣K532

Now when your partner jumps to 3 Spades you add

---

*There is no problem understanding whether partner has all or no Aces when the answer is 5 Clubs. Four Aces are 16 points and all those points show up in the bidding.

your 22 points + his 13 to 15 = 35 to 37. You are interested in a grand slam. You ask your partner for Aces with a jump to 4 No Trump. Partner responds 5 Hearts showing two Aces. That means you have all the Aces. Now you'd like to know how many Kings the partnership holds because you're dreaming of bidding 7. Blackwood has a bid for that, too.

You ask for Kings by bidding 5 No Trump.

The answers go the same way, by the rank of suits:

5NT

with no Kings bid 6♣
with one King bid 6♦
with two Kings bid 6♥
with three Kings bid 6♠
with four Kings bid 6♣

On this hand your partner's answer is 6 Diamonds showing one King. You have all the Aces and all the Kings. You bid 7 Spades.

The Opening Lead Against a Slam

The opening lead against a slam is different from the opening lead against a part-score or game contract.

You make a *safe* lead against a slam. Beware of leading away from a Kxx or a Qxx; the opponents have almost all the points and this might give the declarer a "free" finesse and the one extra trick he needs to make his slam. The best lead usually is the top of a sequence in honors or the top of nothing:

<u>K</u>QJ2   <u>9</u>76

How to Score a Slam

There are three ways to get a big score at bridge, to win a rubber, to double the opponents when they bid too much and set them, and to bid and make a slam. The slam premium is large but it's even larger if you're vulnerable.

	Not Vulnerable	Vulnerable
Little Slam	500	750
Grand Slam	1000	1500

Now you are ready to work the scoring drill at the back of the book. After that you will be able to keep score when you play bridge. A good bridge player is a good scorekeeper.

Tips:

In using Blackwood ask for Kings only if your side has all the Aces.

If you hold all the Aces in your own hand and only need to know about Kings, start with 4 No Trump anyway, then bid 5 No Trump. Jumping to 5 No Trump first would confuse your partner; a confused partner is dangerousssssss!

Beware of asking for Aces when you plan to play in Clubs. The response can catapult you into a slam you don't want to be in. For instance, you're bidding Clubs and if your partner has two Aces you'd try a small slam:

4 NT ☐ 5♦

He just had one but you have to go to six to get out of Diamonds.

V. Slam Bidding Drill

1. How many points does it take to make:

   6NT_____   4♥ _____   5♦ _____   7♣_____

2. Partner opened 1NT, what is your bid?

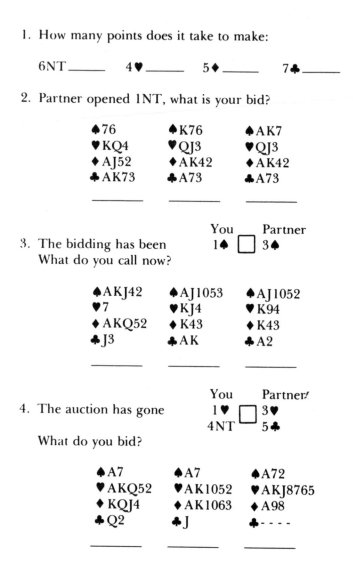

♠76	♠K76	♠AK7
♥KQ4	♥QJ3	♥QJ3
♦AJ52	♦AK42	♦AK42
♣AK73	♣A73	♣A73
_____	_____	_____

3. The bidding has been
   What do you call now?

   You [ ] Partner
   1♠   3♠

♠AKJ42	♠AJ1053	♠AJ1052
♥7	♥KJ4	♥K94
♦AKQ52	♦K43	♦K43
♣J3	♣AK	♣A2
_____	_____	_____

4. The auction has gone

   You [ ] Partner
   1♥   3♥
   4NT   5♣

   What do you bid?

♠A7	♠A7	♠A72
♥AKQ52	♥AK1052	♥AKJ8765
♦KQJ4	♦AK1063	♦A98
♣Q2	♣J	♣- - - -
_____	_____	_____

17. Bidding a Slam

```
              ♠ A943
              ♥ 3
              ♦ 862
              ♣ AKJ86
  ♠106          N          ♠87
  ♥10976                   ♥Q542
  ♦KQJ95    W     E        ♦1074
  ♣103          S          ♣Q974
              ♠ KQJ52
              ♥ AKJ8
              ♦ A3
              ♣ 52
```

South deals
The bidding:

SOUTH	WEST	NORTH	EAST
1 Spade	Pass	3 Spades	Pass
4 NT	Pass	5 Hearts	Pass
5 NT	Pass	6 Diamonds	Pass
6 Spades	Pass	Pass	Pass

South opened the bidding with 1 Spade and North, with trump support and 14 points, jumped to 3 Spades.

South counted his hand at 20 points and realized he was in the slam zone, 20 + 13 = 33. But he wanted to be sure the partnership held three Aces.

He employed Blackwood to find out, bidding 4 No Trump. The answer was 5 Hearts showing two Aces. They had *all* the Aces. He was curious about Kings and asked by bidding 5 No Trump. The response of 6 Diamonds showed one King. South settled for 6 Spades.

West attacked with the King of Diamonds and

declarer saw immediately he had one Diamond loser. He counted five Spades, two Hearts, he could trump two Hearts in dummy, one Diamond trick, and two Club tricks. That was 12 tricks and the slam was coming home.

South took the Diamond Ace and set out to pull the opponents' trumps, leading the King of Spades and then the Queen. All followed so that was attended to. He moved to Clubs.

He was not going to take the Club finesse because he held a doubleton and could trump the third round. South took the Ace and the King of Clubs, led a Club and ruffed.

He played the Ace of Hearts and then the King, followed by a little Heart which he trumped in dummy.

Now declarer led a little Club, the Queen fell, and he trumped it. South led his last Heart and again trumped in dummy. Now he pulled out that good Jack of Clubs from dummy and threw away the losing Diamond from the closed hand. He won the last trick with a trump. South made seven by setting up the Jack of Clubs.

Notice how he trumped a Club in his hand and then trumped a Heart in dummy, then trumped a Club again in his hand? That's called a crossruff because he was crossing from one hand to the other by ruffing.

South could easily go wrong on this hand. If he took the Club finesse he would go down. You never take a finesse you don't have to take.

18. Bidding a Grand

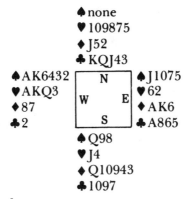

```
              ♠ none
              ♥ 109875
              ♦ J52
              ♣ KQJ43
  ♠ AK6432    ┌─────────┐    ♠ J1075
  ♥ AKQ3      │    N    │    ♥ 62
  ♦ 87        │ W     E │    ♦ AK6
  ♣ 2         │    S    │    ♣ A865
              └─────────┘
              ♠ Q98
              ♥ J4
              ♦ Q10943
              ♣ 1097
```

West deals

The bidding:

WEST	NORTH	EAST	SOUTH
1 Spade	Pass	3 Spades	Pass
4 No Trump	Pass	5 Hearts	Pass
5 No Trump	Pass	6 Diamonds	Pass
7 Spades	Pass	Pass	Pass

West opened his 19-point hand with 1 Spade and his partner jumped to 3. West was slam-minded and asked for Aces. When he found his partner had two West pushed on asking for Kings. Partner had one. West visualized a grand slam with his losing minor cards taken care of. He climbed all the way.

North led the King of Clubs which was won with dummy's Ace. Declarer counted carefully six Spade tricks, three Hearts and a Heart ruff, two Diamonds, one Club = 13. He led a low trump and took the Ace, noticing North couldn't follow suit.

He crossed to dummy with the Diamond King and led the Jack of Spades. South followed low and so did declarer, finessing. Next, another Spade — the Queen fell and Declarer topped it with the King. He cashed three top Hearts and trumped the Heart loser. Now he collected the Ace of Diamonds and claimed the last three tricks with trumps.

When North couldn't follow to Spades he discarded a black Club hoping declarer would see the color but not the suit! But West had his eyes wide open. It was a good ploy, but it didn't fool West that day.

*Mr. Blackwood has his copy of **Bridge Made Easy** autographed by the author. "I never saw a better book for beginners," he declared.*

19. No Trump Slam

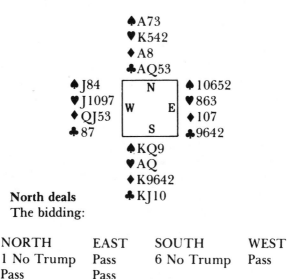

North deals
The bidding:

NORTH	EAST	SOUTH	WEST
1 No Trump	Pass	6 No Trump	Pass
Pass	Pass		

North opened 1 No Trump and South added the partnership assets — 16 + 18 = 34 — and bid 6 No Trump.

From his worthless hand East extracted the Club two. Declarer counted tricks, four Clubs, two Diamonds, three Spades, and three Hearts = 12. His chance for an overtrick lay in Diamonds or Hearts.

He took the Jack of Clubs and then the King, the Ace, and the Queen. Next, the Ace and Queen of Hearts and back to his hand with the Spade Ace to play the King of Hearts. Now he collected the King and Queen of Spades.

That was his tenth trick and West took a long time

to discard. He could no longer protect the Diamond Queen and hold onto the high Heart. West decided to protect the suit he could see in dummy, the Diamonds, and discarded the Heart.

Declarer was a good mathematician. He knew the Heart in his hand was the only one left now. He played the Diamond King and then went over to the Diamond Ace and his tiny 5 of Hearts that had become a winner and his thirteenth trick.

Whenever you want one more trick than you have try the squeeze, cashing all your top tricks. If one hand happens to be protecting two suits, that hand will be squeezed out of one of them. That's what happened to West on this hand. He was helpless.

20. Stopping at Five

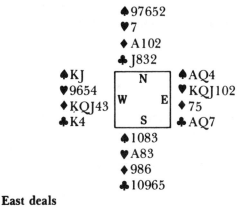

```
              ♠97652
              ♥7
              ♦A102
              ♣J832
♠KJ          ┌─────────┐      ♠AQ4
♥9654        │    N    │      ♥KQJ102
♦KQJ43     W │         │ E    ♦75
♣K4          │    S    │      ♣AQ7
             └─────────┘
              ♠1083
              ♥A83
              ♦986
              ♣10965
```

East deals

The bidding:

EAST	SOUTH	WEST	NORTH
1 Heart	Pass	3 Hearts	Pass
4 No Trump	Pass	5 Clubs	Pass
5 Hearts	Pass	Pass	Pass

East opened 1 Heart and when his partner jumped to 3 East heard a knocking on the slam door. "Four No Trump", he asked and got the bleak reply, "Five Clubs". He signed off with 5 Hearts, thankful for the Blackwood Convention.

South opened the 10 of Clubs. Declarer took the King. He could see four trump tricks, three Spades, three Clubs, and two Diamonds = 12, but the opponents would have to get their two Aces before he could get all his tricks so he knew he'd make only 11.

Declarer led a low Heart from dummy and put in an honor. South held up. He knew he'd always get his

Ace of trumps and he wanted to see what his partner wanted led. Declarer continued the Heart King and South won the Ace as North played a tiny Spade. South remembered his partner played a little Club at trick one. By elimination he chose a Diamond return, the nine, top of nothing. Dummy's Jack pushed out the Ace.

Trying for a Ruff

North returned a Diamond hoping his partner could ruff but South had to follow and dummy's Queen won.

Declarer stopped to pick up the outstanding trump, then he took the Ace and Queen of Clubs, then the three Spade tricks, the King, the Ace, and the Queen. He claimed the last two tricks with trumps, making five.

VI. RESPONDING TO 1 NO TRUMP WITH A LONG SUIT

No Trump contracts are the bargain buy of the bridge table. Tricks count more and it takes fewer of them to make a game than in any other contract.

However, No Trump is the most treacherous contract in bridge. You are more likely to go down than in any other bid. It is wiser to play in a major if you have a trump suit. It takes the same number of high card points, 26, to make 4 Hearts or 4 Spades as it does to make 3 No Trump.

With a Six-Card Major

When your partner opens 1 No Trump and you have an unbalanced hand with a six-card Heart or Spade suit and 10 or more points in high cards and distribution, jump to game in your suit.

♠AJ9874   ♥8   ♦A752   ♣85

At No Trump your hand is worth only nine points and the singleton Heart looks ominous. The opponents might drive out your partner's Heart "stop", run the suit, and set him.

Now, how does that hand look at Spades? You have an eight-card trump suit because partner had to have at least two Spades to open a No Trump. What's the point count at Spades? The singleton and doubleton become assets worth three points. The hand adds up to 12. Partner has to have a minimum of 16 to open a No Trump, 16 + 12 = 28. You see a game in Spades so you jump to 4 Spades. You won't have to worry about those Hearts; you can trump them.

With a Five-Card Major

When your partner opens a No Trump and you have an unbalanced hand worth 10 or more points but only five cards in your long major, jump the bidding but only to 3.

♠9   ♥AQJ84   ♦Q982   ♣J73

In this hand you aren't sure you have an eight-card trump suit. Partner could have bid 1 No Trump with only two Hearts. When you jump to 3 Hearts you're saying, "We want to play this hand in game. I'd rather play it in Hearts but I'm not positive we have a trump suit. If you have three of my Hearts please bid 4 Hearts. If you only have two, bid 3 No Trump."

With a Long Minor

Suppose your partner opens a No Trump and you have an unbalanced hand with a long minor and 10 or more high card points. That's a different story. It takes so many tricks to make a game in Diamonds or Clubs it's better to play the No Trump contract. You conceal a long minor and jump to 3 No Trump.

♠Kxx   ♥x   ♦AKJxx   ♣xxxx

If you played this hand at Diamonds you'd need 11 tricks for a game. If your partner played at No Trump he'd only need nine. It's easier to get nine than 11. Gamble it out, bid 3 No Trump.

Suppose your hand didn't include the King of Spades:

♠872　　♥10　　♦AKJ94　　♣8753

You have eight high-card points and your bid is 2 NT.

♠872　　♥10　　♦AKJ942　　♣875

With a six-card minor headed by two or three top honors jump to 3 No Trump, hoping the long suit will bring home the contract. In this hand your partner is more likely to have the Queen of Diamonds than anybody at the table; if he doesn't he has three small ones and the Queen is likely to fall. There is an excellent chance of taking six Diamond tricks.

A long suit is an advantage at No Trump, especially when you have honors in it to help set up the small cards. So you try a game with one or two fewer points.

The Rescue Bid

Opposite a No Trump opening what do you do with an unbalanced hand, a long suit, and a weak hand of seven points or less?

♠J109876　　♥8　　♦Q972　　♣83

At No Trump you have only three points but at Spades your singleton and doubleton add value to your hand and it's worth six points. That's twice as much. At No Trump your hand probably won't produce a single trick but at Spades it will take at least three.

The opening No Trump bidder usually has three and a half tricks in his hand. He's dependent on getting to dummy to make his finesses. He won't be able to. You have a much better chance of making 2 Spades than your partner has of making 1 No Trump because at Spades you can get to your hand with trumps.

You rescue your partner by bidding 2 Spades. You don't jump so this announces a weak hand and warns partner not to bid any more. People who have never studied bridge go wrong on this one.

The bids of 2 Spades, 2 Hearts and 2 Diamonds are rescues. (In another course some day, you'll study a special meaning for the bid of 2 Clubs.)

Leading Toward an Honor

When you have K3 ☐ Q2, you are sure to get a trick in that suit because the King will force the play of the Ace and now the Queen is high.

What happens when you have K3 ☐ 72? Can you still get a trick? Yes, if the Ace is in the "right" spot:

Who has the Ace of Clubs? If your left-hand opponent has it, you can always take a trick by leading *toward* the King. If he plays the Ace you'll play the 3 and your King will be high. If he plays low, you play the King and it wins. If West is an experienced player he will usually play a low card hoping you will lose your nerve and play the 3. But you reach over and pick up the King and play it. It's now or never. You know they won't give it to you on the next go-round when it's all alone. It's a 50 per cent proposition. Half the time the Ace will be dealt to West, half the time to East, so half the time you'll win a trick with the King.

It's a similar story if you have KQ3. If the Ace is "right" you can get two tricks:

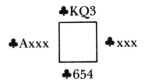

You lead toward the big card, so you lead from your hand. If West plays low, you play the Queen. If that wins the trick you come back to your hand in another suit and lead the 5. Now West will see you know how to play your cards and will go up with the Ace. You'll play the 3. Your King is the ranking Club. You won two tricks because the person with the Ace had to play before you had to put up a big card.

Flash Card

Responding to 1 NT, unbalanced hand

1 NT ☐

With 0-7 and a 5- or 6-card suit *rescue* with 2♦, 2♥, 2♠

With 10 and a 5-card major *jump* to 3♥ or 3♠*

With 10 and a 6-card major *jump* to 4♥, 4♠

With 10 and a long minor conceal the minor, bid 3 NT; with 8 or 9 bid 2 NT

*Opener responds 3 NT with two-card support. Takes you to 4 with three-card support.

VI. Suit Responses to 1 NT Drill

1. What is the point count of these hands and what is your opening bid?

♠AKJ6	♠AQ6	♠AK62	♠KJ52
♥AK72	♥AK2	♥AQ2	♥QJ10
♦Q74	♦Q97	♦76	♦KQ4
♣98	♣K987	♣KJ54	♣AK5

2. Your partner opened 1 NT. What is your response?

♠Q93	♠AJ9432	♠Q9852	♠982
♥K42	♥K109	♥AK4	♥QJ10862
♦A94	♦8	♦8	♦82
♣10832	♣K75	♣K752	♣98

♠K65	♠Q93
♥K63	♥K42
♦8764	♦AJ4
♣953	♣10832

3. The bidding went:

	You	Partner
	1 NT	3H
	?	

What is your rebid with:

♠AJ42	♠AQ32	♠AQ32
♥KQ5	♥KQ	♥J72
♦Q32	♦Q932	♦KQ3
♣A94	♣A94	♣A94

21. Rescue the One No Trump Bidder

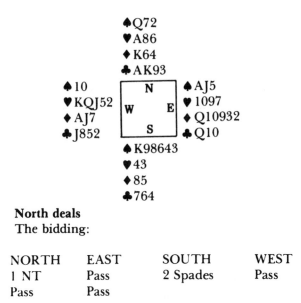

```
              ♠Q72
              ♥A86
              ♦K64
              ♣AK93
  ♠10          ┌─────────┐    ♠AJ5
  ♥KQJ52       │   N     │    ♥1097
  ♦AJ7        W│         │E   ♦Q10932
  ♣J852        │   S     │    ♣Q10
               └─────────┘
              ♠K98643
              ♥43
              ♦85
              ♣764
```

North deals
The bidding:

NORTH	EAST	SOUTH	WEST
1 NT	Pass	2 Spades	Pass
Pass	Pass		

North was excited when he saw his 16-point hand and made his opening bid of 1 No Trump. But as sometimes happens at the bridge table when one partner gets a big hand, the other one gets a weak hand. South had only three high-card points. At No Trump this hand *might* produce one trick but with Spades as trumps it would take several. A rescue was called for and South bid 2 Spades. This was bad news for North but he trusted his partner and passed. North knew only a jump in a suit shows interest in game.

West opened the top of his sequence in honors, the King of Hearts. The dummy came down and declarer counted four or five Spade tricks, one Heart, two Clubs, and maybe one Diamond if the Ace was right. That was seven sure's and two maybe's.

Declarer went up with the Ace of Hearts and attacked trumps, leading the 2 of Spades from dummy. East played low; he wanted bigger game for his Ace. South played the King and won. He continued with the 3 of Spades and West discarded the 2 of Hearts. It didn't matter what came from dummy; East had two trump tricks. South chose the Queen and East topped it with the Ace and took the Jack of Spades. Next he returned his partner's suit, leading the 10 of Hearts and it won. East continued the 9 of Hearts but Declarer trumped.

South realized he was down unless the Ace of Diamonds was with West; he played the 8 of Diamonds, leading *toward* the big card. West played the 7, and the declarer pulled out the King from dummy. It won. Now South cashed the Ace and the King of Clubs, gave up a Club and a Diamond, and made the rest of the tricks. He scored 60 below the line.

(You might like to re-play this hand at No Trump. With careful play North can win five or six tricks. He won't be able to get to the Spade suit because East will hold up the Ace. That's down one, at least. For this hand it was two tricks better to play Spades.)

22. Preferring a Major

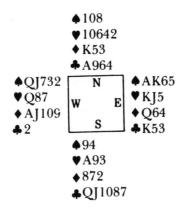

♠ 108
♥ 10642
♦ K53
♣ A964

♠ QJ732   ♠ AK65
♥ Q87   ♥ KJ5
♦ AJ109   ♦ Q64
♣ 2   ♣ K53

♠ 94
♥ A93
♦ 872
♣ QJ1087

East deals
The bidding:

EAST	SOUTH	WEST	NORTH
1 NT	Pass	3 Spades	Pass
4 Spades	Pass	Pass	Pass

East opened 1 No Trump with his 16 points and perfectly balanced hand. West frowned at his club singleton and jumped to 3 Spades. East had a fit and bid 4.

North led the 3 of Diamonds and declarer let it ride to his 9. Declarer counted five Spade tricks, two Hearts, and three or four Diamonds = 10 or 11. He led the Queen of Spades and then the Jack, gathering in all the enemy trumps.

He decided to try to steal the King of Clubs! He led the 2; North hated to put his Ace on such a tiny one so he began a signal with the 9. Declarer picked up the King and laid it on the table. South followed with the 10.

Declarer's timing was perfect. A swindle is more likely to succeed early in a hand before the opponents get wise to the distribution.

Now West led the King of Hearts which was snared by South's Ace. South returned his partner's opening lead, playing his top Diamond. Declarer followed with the 10 and North won his King.

Remembering his partner's high Club North decided to take his Ace but declarer ruffed. Then West took the Ace and Jack of Diamonds, the Queen and Jack of Hearts, and had two good trumps to boot. He made five.

Played at No Trump East would get a Club lead and eventually lose four Clubs and the Ace of Hearts, down one.

23. Jumping to Four Spades

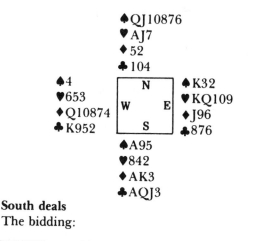

♠QJ10876
♥AJ7
♦52
♣104

♠4
♥653
♦Q10874
♣K952

♠K32
♥KQ109
♦J96
♣876

♠A95
♥842
♦AK3
♣AQJ3

South deals
The bidding:

SOUTH	WEST	NORTH	EAST
1 NT	Pass	4 Spades	Pass
Pass	Pass		

One No Trump South bid, on top of his call with 18 points. North jumped to the safer game of 4 Spades.

East led the King of Hearts. Declarer stopped to count five Spade tricks, one Heart, two Diamonds, and three Clubs = 11. Before he could get all those he could lose the King of trumps, two Hearts, and a Club. That would put him down.

The Bath Coup*

On the King of Hearts declarer played dummy's 2, West played the 3 and declarer the 7. This is an old card play from the days of Whist and is called the Bath Coup.

*See page vi.

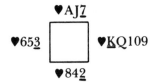

♥AJ7

♥653   ♥KQ109

♥842

Now if East continues the suit declarer will win two tricks. If East leads the Queen the Ace will take it and the Jack will be high. If he leads low declarer will take it with the Jack.

East studied the cards and looked at partner's 3 of Hearts. That wasn't promising any big card. East switched to the 8 of Clubs. Declarer finessed and lost to the King.

West went back to Hearts, leading the 6, top of nothing. North went up with the Ace.

Declarer wanted to finesse for the King of trumps. He led the Queen of Spades, East followed low and so did everyone else. Now declarer tried again with the Jack, again East was low, again declarer won. Now the Ace of Spades picked up the King.

Declarer was home. He shifted to Clubs, playing the Ace, then the Queen on which he discarded that losing Heart. Then he picked up his Ace and King of Diamonds. He had three top Spades left. He made five, losing the King of Hearts and the King of Clubs.

If he had taken the first Heart he would make only four because he'd lose the timing on the hand. When West collected the King of Clubs he would shoot back a Heart and East would get two Heart tricks instead of one.

24. Concealing a Long Minor

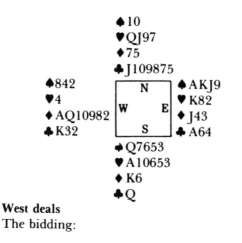

```
                    ♠ 10
                    ♥ QJ97
                    ♦ 75
                    ♣ J109875
      ♠ 842            N          ♠ AKJ9
      ♥ 4                         ♥ K82
      ♦ AQ10982    W       E      ♦ J43
      ♣ K32                       ♣ A64
                    S
                    ♠ Q7653
                    ♥ A10653
                    ♦ K6
                    ♣ Q
```

West deals
The bidding:

WEST	NORTH	EAST	SOUTH
Pass	Pass	1 NT	Pass
3 NT	Pass	Pass	Pass

East started activities with 1 No Trump and West ignored the long minor suit and jumped to game. He only had nine points but he took some credit for his long Diamonds.

South got off with his fourth best Heart, the 5. He figured his Hearts had more potential than his Spades. North put up the Jack and declarer snapped up his King.

Praying the Diamonds would finesse he laid down the Jack and breathed a sigh of relief when it held. Now another Diamond and the King fell to the Ace. Declarer ran a stream of Diamonds discarding two useless Hearts and a Club from the closed hand.

He played the Ace and King of Clubs, then resisted the Spade finesse and cashed the Ace and King of Spades. That gave him 11 tricks and left South to collect the Queen of Spades and Ace of Hearts.

VII. THE TAKE-OUT DOUBLE

When you overcall you're announcing that you have a good five-card suit and 10 to 15 points. Suppose you don't have a good five-card suit, but you have a good hand. What can you do? Suppose your right-hand opponent opened 1 Heart and your hand was:

♠K972   ♥92   ♦AQ63   ♣KQ3

With 14 high-card points you certainly want to get in the auction. If the Ace of Diamonds had been a Spade you'd overcall 1 Spade. Since you don't have a suit to overcall you say, "Double". This is a special bid and it is called a take-out double. It means just what the name implies. You are saying, *Partner, please take me out of this double by bidding your longest suit. I have at least an opening hand and I can help you in any suit except the one already bid by the opponent.*

The take-out double is a bidding tactic that enables you to show strength and at the same time force your partner to name his best suit. It requires:

1. The equivalent of an opening bid;
2. Support for all unbid suits; or
3. A suit of your own with 16 points or more.

A take-out double asks your partner to name the trump suit for you. You would always rather for him to select a major suit because that is the easiest route to game. Therefore you assure him you have support in an unbid major.

Here are some other examples of a take-out double after an opponent opened 1 Heart:

1.	♠K432	♥5	♦AK76	♣AJ54
2.	♠Q1053	♥-	♦AK1076	♣A1076
3.	♠AK983	♥76	♦AJ54	♣A2

On the first hand you have help in all three of the unbid suits but no biddable suit of your own.

On the second hand you don't want to overcall 2 Diamonds because your partner might be able to bid Spades and you want to leave that option open.

On the third hand you're too strong with 16 high-card points to overcall 1 Spade. An overcall at the 1 level shows 10 to 15 points and at the 2 level, 13 to 15 points. The take-out double begins where overcalling ends. With bigger hands you make a take-out double — even though you have a suit — and bid your suit on the next round. When you ask your partner to name the trump suit and then you change the suit, you're showing a big hand and your partner can raise you on very little. If your partner happened to bid your suit you can give a raise with 16 or more.

Responding to a Take-Out Double

Now let's look at this bid from another seat at the table. Suppose the dealer bid a Heart and your partner doubled for take-out. You have to name the trump suit. What would you bid with:

♠J765	♥654	♦987	♣765

You have a terrible hand but you must not pass. The

opponents would be delighted to play 1 Heart doubled because they could make it and get extra score for fulfilling a doubled contract. Your partner asked you to bid your longest suit and especially promised you support in the unbid major. Bid 1 Spade. Your partner has *forced* you to bid and knows it's possible you are broke. He has to have a lot of power to push further.

♠AJ76   ♥543   ♦AJ63   ♣98

Here you have a better hand. Since you had to bid whether you had anything or not, *jump the bidding one round when you have 10 points.* Bid 2 Spades.

♠AKJ7   ♥543   ♦AJ65   ♣65

Here you have an opening hand yourself and again help in that unbid major. Jump right to game, say 4 Spades. Your partner said he had help in Spades and he said he had 13 points. It's simple arithmetic. You see game and you bid it.

You Don't Have the Other Major

Sometimes your partner will make a take-out double and you won't have help in the other major. In fact, most of your points are in the suit the opponent bid. Suppose your partner doubles 1 Heart, and your hand is:

♠Q72   ♥AJ7   ♦J987   ♣1042

Bid 1 No Trump. This bid shows a sure trick in the opponent's suit (preferably two) and eight to 10 high-card points. You would jump to 2 No Trump with 11 or 12.

♠982   ♥543   ♦J10985   ♣52

When you can't bid a major or No Trump you will have to settle for a minor. On this hand say 2 Diamonds. This denies four cards in the Spade suit and it denies 10 points since you didn't jump.

Responding After a Double

Let's move now to a different seat at the table. Your partner opened with 1 Heart and the next person made a take-out double. What happens to you?

Double

1♥ ?

If you have 10 high card points or more you say, "Redouble." This bid tells your partner that your side has most of the points, the opponents are headed for a shaky contract, and you might want to make a penalty double. You're asking him to let you make the next bid for the partnership.

Any other bid shows fewer than 10 high card points. You may pass, raise your partner's suit, name a new suit, or bid No Trump.

THE PENALTY DOUBLE

There are two uses of the bid "Double". One is for take-out and the other is to penalize the opponents when they bid too much. It is easy to tell which your partner means. When a double is a take-out double, it is made (1) at a player's first opportunity to bid, and (2) partner must not have made a bid.

When it is made at any other time it is a penalty double. Your partner thinks the opponents won't make their contract and hopes to get a lot of score by setting them.

In considering a penalty double count the tricks you expect to win, add those partner is expected to take, and if the total is sufficient to set the contract *two tricks* let the ax fall. (Allow a one trick leeway in case of an unlucky lay of the cards.) One trick should be in the trump suit.

If partner opened one of a suit figure him for two tricks; if he opened one No Trump count on him for three and a half tricks; if he made an overcall expect one trick.

Flash Cards

Responding to a Take-Out Double

Double

Dealer: 1♥ ☐ Pass

?

Name your best suit at lowest level
Prefer an unbid major
With 10 points jump one level
With 13 points go to game
With a trick in opponent's suit and
   8-10 bid 1 NT
   11-12 jump to 2 NT
   13 jump to 3 NT

Responding *after* a Take-Out Double

Double
1♥ ☐ ? Redouble with 10 high card pts.
            Any other bid shows fewer.

VII. The Take-Out Double Drill

1. Your right-hand opponent opened 1♥. What do you bid?

♠AQJ72	♠AQJ10	♠AQ98	♠98
♥65	♥65	♥65	♥AQJ42
♦AQ4	♦AQ4	♦AK7642	♦A762
♣932	♣K932	♣3	♣103

——— ——— —— ———

♠84	♠J6
♥92	♥A5
♦AQJ105	♦AKQ1076
♣KJ92	♣A72

——— ———

2. Your opponent opened one Club. What's your bid?

♠AQJ4	♠AQJ104	♠AKJ94
♥KJ103	♥KQ42	♥32
♦K102	♦K93	♦Q93
♣94	♣4	♣876

——— ——— ———

3. The bidding went:

| East | Partner | West | You |
| 1♦ | Double | Pass | ? |

What do you bid with:

♠1098	♠KJ109	♠K109	♠K42
♥863	♥K63	♥K76	♥KJ1094
♦J762	♦8	♦QJ42	♦A2
♣987	♣Q8762	♣1096	♣Q73

——— ——— ——— ———

25. The Take-Out Double

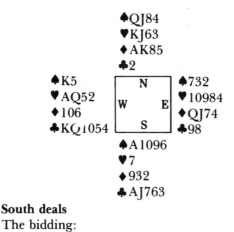

♠QJ84
♥KJ63
♦AK85
♣2

♠K5   ♠732
♥AQ52   ♥10984
♦106   ♦QJ74
♣KQ1054   ♣98

♠A1096
♥7
♦932
♣AJ763

South deals
The bidding:

SOUTH	WEST	NORTH	EAST
Pass	1 Club	Double	Pass
2 Spades	Pass	4 Spades	

West opened 1 Club and North doubled. This double was a take-out double because North made it at his first opportunity and his partner had never bid. Suddenly, South liked his hand — four cards in Spades and 9 highs + 2 distributional points. He jumped to 2 spades. With his 16 count North climbed to game.

West stepped out with the King of Clubs and then the dummy came down. South knew most of the high cards out against him were in the West hand because West made an opening bid and his partner didn't chirp.

Declarer reasoned the King of trumps was on the wrong side and he was going to lose it. However, the

Ace of Hearts was in the right place so he could lead toward the King and win a trick. Nevertheless, he could only find three Spade tricks and a ruff, one Heart, two Diamonds, and one Club. Eight tricks were not enough.

The Crossruff

Whenever dummy has a singleton in one suit and the declarer a singleton in another suit it is generally profitable not to draw trumps at all but to crossruff the hand. That is, in this hand, to ruff Clubs in dummy and Hearts in the closed hand, crossing back and forth, winning the trumps separately.

Playing this way the bookkeeping process was two Diamond tricks, one Club, one Heart, two Hearts ruffed, three Clubs ruffed, and the Ace of Spades = 10. That's enough!

South took his Ace of Clubs and then laid down his singleton Heart. West jumped up with his Ace and returned the 10 of Diamonds. Declarer won the King.

Take Side Winners First

Whenever a declarer attempts a crossruff he first takes his winners in the side suits. This is to prevent the opponents from discarding in these suits during the cross-ruffing, enabling them later to trump declarer's good cards.

So South collected the Ace of Diamonds, and the King of Hearts (on which he dropped a losing Diamond). Now the hand was ready for the crossruff.

Declarer led a low Heart from dummy and trumped in his hand with a little Spade; a low Club from declarer's hand was trumped in dummy; a Heart back and trumped; a Club over and trumped. Next, a Diamond from dummy trumped with the 10 of Spades but West, also out of Diamonds, over-ruffed with the Spade King.

Defense Against a Crossruff

When the defenders see a declarer trying to make all his trumps separately on a crossruff, their best strategy is to lead trumps, pulling two of declarer's trumps together.

So West returned the 5 of Spades and the Ace won. Then declarer led a Club and ruffed with the board's Queen. East had the only trump and won the last trick.

If you re-play the hand and draw trumps first you'll only win eight tricks, just four trump tricks, and you'll go down two. Declarer won two more tricks because he had the type of hand where he could use his trumps separately.

Tip

In most suit contracts, the first step declarer takes is to pull the opponents' trumps. In a few cases it is better to delay the leading of trumps, or never lead trumps at all, as in this crossruff. Consider a crossruff when you have a singleton or void in your hand, and your dummy is short in another suit.

26. Landing in a No Trump Game

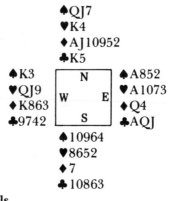

West deals
The bidding:

WEST	NORTH	EAST	SOUTH
Pass	1 Diamond	Double	Pass
1 NT	Pass	2 NT	Pass
3 NT	Pass	Pass	Pass

When East's take-out double brought a No Trump bid from his partner, East saw there was hope of a game, 17 + 8 = 25. When he bid 2 NT he invited his partner to go to game if he was on the top of his bid. West had nine points so he went to game.

North's best chance to set the contract rested in the Diamond suit. He chose to lead the Jack, the top of an interior sequence.

When the dummy came down with 17 points North's hand became an open book. All the outstanding 14 points stood to be with North. West saw he'd be able to successfully finesse for the missing King of Hearts and King of Clubs. He added his tricks: four Hearts, three Clubs, two Spades, and one Diamond = 10.

The Queen of Diamonds won the first trick. Declarer came to his hand with the King of Spades to take the Heart finesse. He led the Heart Queen, North topped it with the King, and dummy's Ace won. Now back to the Heart 9 to try the Club finesse. A low Club was led toward the Jack and when it won no one was surprised.

A little Heart was played back to the Jack to get in the correct hand for another Club finesse. The second Club was led, the King fell, and the Ace covered it. Now declarer collected the Queen of Clubs and the 10 of Hearts, making nine tricks. He took the Ace of Spades for his tenth trick. He exited with a low Spade which North won with the Queen. Eventually, North had to lead Diamonds around to declarer's King. That gave West 11 tricks. It's easier to play a hand when you can figure from the bidding where the big cards are.

Tip

Usually we take all our tricks in one suit before we switch to another but in this hand West needed to save his Hearts for entries so he could finesse Clubs twice.

27. How High To Go?

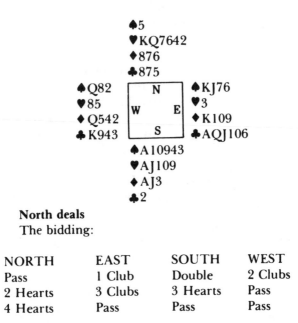

♠5
♥KQ7642
♦876
♣875

♠Q82
♥85
♦Q542
♣K943

N
W E
S

♠KJ76
♥3
♦K109
♣AQJ106

♠A10943
♥AJ109
♦AJ3
♣2

North deals
The bidding:

NORTH	EAST	SOUTH	WEST
Pass	1 Club	Double	2 Clubs
2 Hearts	3 Clubs	3 Hearts	Pass
4 Hearts	Pass	Pass	Pass

East opened a Club and South made a take-out double. He didn't want to overcall Spades because he didn't have two of the three top honors. He had support for the unbid suits. West muddied the waters with a Club raise. This took North off the hook and he no longer had to respond to his partner's double. But he liked his suit and came in freely with 2 Hearts. East made it 3 Clubs and South raised to 3 Hearts. North looked at his long suit and decided to try a game.

East led the Club Ace. West noted dummy's single Club but he could see no desirable switch so he suggested another Club by playing the 9. However, East pulled out a trump.

Declarer figured to win six Hearts, two Club ruffs, one Spade and one Diamond = 10. The only possibility for another was to set up a Spade.

North won the Heart 9, laid down the Ace of Spades and ruffed a Spade. He crossed back to dummy with a trump. Now the opponents were out of Hearts. Another Spade was led and trumped and a Club ruffed in dummy. A fourth Spade was pulled from the board and trumped in the closed hand and the King crashed.

Now a Diamond was played to the Ace and declarer collected the good 10 of Spades, discarding a losing Diamond from the closed hand. He conceded a Diamond and took his good trump. He brought in 11 tricks, eight with Hearts.

28. Double Trouble

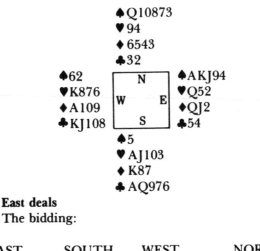

♠ Q10873
♥ 94
♦ 6543
♣ 32

♠ 62
♥ K876
♦ A109
♣ KJ108

♠ AKJ94
♥ Q52
♦ QJ2
♣ 54

♠ 5
♥ AJ103
♦ K87
♣ AQ976

East deals
The bidding:

EAST	SOUTH	WEST	NORTH
1 Spade	Double	Redouble	Pass
Pass	2 Clubs	Double	Pass
Pass	Pass		

East bid a Spade and South doubled hoping his partner could bid Hearts. West had 11 highs and proclaimed it with a redouble. North was no longer forced to bid because the redouble gave his partner another chance at the auction. He passed. East loved 1 Spade doubled and redoubled; he passed. South ran to 2 Clubs. West liked the opponent's suit better than he liked his partner's so he doubled; this was for penalties because his partner had made a bid. All passed.

West started his partner's suit, leading the Spade 6, top of a doubleton. Declarer could see he had to face the music. He had so few trick possibilities he couldn't count them. He set out to do the best he could.

Declarer covered with dummy's Spade 7 (it didn't matter) and East carefully played the 9 which held.

When your partner doubles a low-level contract he usually likes a trump lead. It was the meanest play East could make. He led the 5 of Clubs, declarer barely covered, and West claimed the trick with the 8.

West returned the Spade 2, low from dummy, covered by East, and declarer won with the trump 7.

Declarer played a low Heart to the 9 and it rode around to East's Queen. East found another trump lead (now declarer couldn't ruff a Heart in dummy) and declarer took the Ace of Clubs. He played the Ace of Hearts, and then the Jack of Hearts. West won with the King.

West's safest return was a Heart and declarer got the 10. Declarer led a low Diamond. West's 9 was high, but East overtook with the Jack to return a Diamond. Now West won two Diamond tricks but he finally had to lead Clubs into declarer's hand, giving South the Queen.

Declarer brought in three Club tricks and two Hearts, going down three doubled.

The play was delicate at moments and South might have picked up one or more tricks against different defense but the hand was hopeless. It's difficult to play with a dead dummy.

Despite the results South made the proper bid. You're going to go down some in bridge. Being too cautious doesn't pay in the long run. Swap the North and West hands and South's double would uncover a game in Hearts.

Tips on Ethics

All bids are made in the same tone of voice. It is improper for a player to double in one tone for take-out and then raise his voice when the double is for penalties.

It is not honorable to describe a bid saying, "I *think* I'll bid 1 Club," as though you're not quite sure. Just say, "1 Club."

It is not proper etiquette for a player to review the bidding for himself. When it's his turn to bid he may ask an opponent to review the bidding for him. Then there's no doubt about inflections of the voice conveying meanings.

Ethics, like many techniques at the card table, have to be learned. Generally the finer the player the higher the ethics.

VIII. MORE RESPONSES TO A MAJOR

When your partner opens 1 Heart or 1 Spade and you have trump support, you give a single raise with 6-10 and a jump raise with 13-15.

What do you do with 11 or 12? It's too much for a single raise and not enough for a jump. The way to show this in-between hand is to make two bids — name a new suit and then give a raise. It's called "The 11-12 Principle." Here's how it works. Your partner opens 1 Heart and you hold:

♠AJ974   ♥A65   ♦52   ♣Q65

You have 12 points, 11 highs + 1 distributional. You bid 1 Spade which forces your partner to bid again. When the bidding comes around next time, you'll complete your description with a raise in Hearts. The bidding might go:

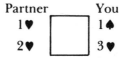

Partner   You
1♥   1♠
2♥   3♥

Then your partner will add 11 or 12 points to his hand. If he opened on 13 he will pass but if he has 14 or 15 he will go to game, 14 + 12 = 26.

If your partner's rebid is in a new suit the bidding is more delicate. You now have to jump to show the raise.

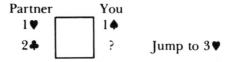

Jump to 3♥

If you bid only 2 Hearts it would sound as though you were saying, "If you want me to *choose* between your two suits I prefer Hearts." You want to show a *raise*, not just a preference, and that requires a jump.

Opener Chooses His Rebid

When you bid 1 Spade your partner has to bid again. When the responder changes the suit it is forcing on the opener. The opener has a variety of choices for his rebid and he wants to choose the one that best describes his distribution and his points.

Scientific Bidding

With a minimum, 13 to 15:
- Opener rebids his suit with six cards;
- Opener gives a single raise with four-card support;
- Opener bids a new suit lower in rank than his first;
- With even distribution bids 1 No Trump.

With a medium hand, 16 to 18:
- With a good six-card suit jumps in his suit;
- With four-card support he can jump raise his partner's suit;
- Bid a new four-card suit lower in rank than his first one. (With even distribution he would have opened 1 NT)

With a maximum, 19 to 21:
- Jump to game in partner's suit with four-card support;

- Jump in a new suit which is forcing to game;
- With even distribution and 19 jump to 2 NT, with 20 or 21 jump to 3 NT.

When you are the opener and you are choosing your rebid it helps to ask, "What can I bid to paint the clearest picture of my hand?" Occasionally you won't be able to find a bid that tells the truth about your point count *and* your distribution. In such cases it is wise to be faithful to the point count.

Three Weak Responses

Suppose when your partner opened 1 Heart you held a weak hand. You struggle to keep the auction open with as few as six measly points in case he has a big hand. There are three responses you can make with 6-10 points. They differ in the number of trumps you have.

Without trump support you bid 1 No Trump.

With normal trump support you give a single raise.

With lots of trumps, good distribution, and not more than nine high-card points you make a triple jump to 4. This type of hand is called a weak-freak.

♠7   ♥QJ543   ♦KQ763   ♣65

This hand is certainly weak but it is a freak because it will take lots of tricks at a Heart contract with its abundance of trumps to handle the two short suits. It is almost worthless if Spades or Clubs are trumps.

You jump to 4 Hearts. This bid describes a hand rich in trumps (usually five or six), rich in distribution (a singleton or a void), and poor in high cards.

The object of this immediate leap to game is to shut out the opponents, to get the bidding so high they will have a hard time exchanging information about their point count and distribution. If your partner has a good hand he will make the contract. If he goes down the opponents probably have missed a game or a part-score. Either way it's a winning bid.

Flash Cards

Raising Partner with Trump Support

1♥ ☐

with 6-10 bid 2♥
with 11-12 bid a new suit and then raise
with 13-15 jump to 3♥, forcing to game.

All Weak Bids

1♥ ☐

Bid 1 NT with 6-9, fewer than 3 trumps
Bid 2♥ with 6-10, and three trumps
Bid 4♥ with five or more trumps, a singleton or a void, and 6-9.

VIII. Responses to a Major Drill

1. Partner opened one Heart. What is your point count and bid?

♠ A7	♠ 94	♠ J76	♠ 6
♥ K632	♥ QJ32	♥ 76	♥ A76532
♦ 654	♦ 43	♦ Q7654	♦ 8
♣ 7654	♣ AQJ56	♣ A53	♣ K9642

_____ _____ _____

2. You opened one Heart and your partner bid one Spade. Choose your re-bid, noting a minimum, medium, or maximum hand:

♠ 9	♠ 8	♠ KJ72	♠ J2
♥ AKJ762	♥ AKJ74	♥ A5432	♥ AJ965
♦ KJ32	♦ 76	♦ A4	♦ AK9
♣ 54	♣ KJ765	♣ 76	♣ AQ3

_____ _____ _____ _____

♠ K4	♠ 8	♠ 1043	♠ 8
♥ A8654	♥ AQJ96	♥ A7642	♥ KJ853
♦ KQ2	♦ A4	♦ QJ2	♦ AQ76
♣ AKQ	♣ KQJ72	♣ AK	♣ K54

_____ _____ _____ _____

♠ 8	♠ QJ63	♠ K2
♥ K9842	♥ KQJ54	♥ AKQ765
♦ AKQ4	♦ AK	♦ 53
♣ A82	♣ 32	♣ A82

_____ _____ _____

29. The Weak-Freak

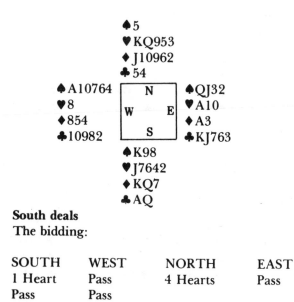

♠ 5
♥ KQ953
♦ J10962
♣ 54

♠ A10764
♥ 8
♦ 854
♣ 10982

♠ QJ32
♥ A10
♦ A3
♣ KJ763

♠ K98
♥ J7642
♦ KQ7
♣ AQ

South deals
The bidding:

SOUTH	WEST	NORTH	EAST
1 Heart	Pass	4 Hearts	Pass
Pass	Pass		

South opened 1 Heart and his partner made the dramatic triple-jump to 4 Hearts. East squirmed in his chair, pondered his 15 high-card points, finally passed.

West opened the 10 of Clubs. Declarer paused to count his winners. With the lead coming into his hand he'd take two Club tricks, then four Diamonds and four Hearts. That was his contract.

South brought in the first trick with the Club Queen. He led a low Heart toward dummy's Queen and East tossed on the Ace. East shifted to the Diamond Ace but was discouraged from continuing the suit by his partner's play of the Diamond 4. He switched to the Queen of

Spades, covered by the King, and won by West's Ace. West returned a Diamond and declarer took the Queen.

South drew the outstanding trump. He collected the King of Diamonds and played a little Spade which he ruffed in dummy. Now he led the good Jack of Diamonds and threw away his losing Spade. He took the Club Ace and showed three trumps in his hand to claim the last three tricks, making 4 Hearts.

This hand was played in an International Championship match between the Italians and the Americans. The bidding, lead, and play went as shown at both tables. East-West had a game in Spades but the bidding got too high for even the experts to find it. North's jump crowded them out of the bidding.

30. Opener Rebids 1 NT

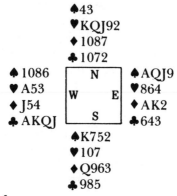

```
              ♠43
              ♥KQJ92
              ♦1087
              ♣1072
  ♠1086     ┌─────────┐   ♠AQJ9
  ♥A53      │   N     │   ♥864
  ♦J54      │ W     E │   ♦AK2
  ♣AKQJ     │   S     │   ♣643
            └─────────┘
              ♠K752
              ♥107
              ♦Q963
              ♣985
```

West deals
The bidding.

WEST	NORTH	EAST	SOUTH
1 Club	Pass	1 Spade	Pass
1 NT	Pass	3 NT	Pass
Pass	Pass		

West began with 1 Club and East sought a major fit by bidding 1 Spade. West rebid 1 No Trump to show his minimum hand with even distribution. East had the same, added his 14 points to his partner's hand and jumped to 3 No Trump.

The Hold-Up Play

North stepped out with the Heart King. Declarer sat silently counting, four Clubs, two Diamonds, three Spades, one Heart = 10 tricks. Then he saw a cloud in the sky — suppose when he took the Spade finesse it lost to South and South returned a Heart to his partner.

Now, North could run his suit and if he held four more Hearts he could set the contract.

With this fear in mind West decided to hold up his Ace of Hearts hoping to deplete South's hand of Hearts so he wouldn't have one to return.

So the King of Hearts held and North continued with the Queen which also won. Now the Jack of Hearts was led and captured by the declarer's Ace, South showing out.

Declarer played the 10 of Spades, dummy's 9 went under it, and South took the King. South was anxious to get his partner in the lead so he could take those Hearts. He recalled the bridge axiom,

> "When dummy's on your right
> Lead the weakest suit in sight.
> When dummy's on your left
> Lead through heft."

South switched to a Club, dummy's weakest suit, but Declarer had everything. He took the Jack of Clubs and followed with the Ace, King, and Queen of Clubs. Now he crossed to dummy to win the Spade Ace, Queen, and Jack. Last he picked up the Ace and King of Diamonds. That made 10 tricks.

The hold-up play was crucial. Suppose declarer had taken the first Heart. When South won the Spade King he'd have a Heart to return and North would collect a total of four Heart tricks, setting declarer one trick. The strategic hold-up gave North the first two tricks with Hearts but kept him from getting two more.

31. Jump Rebid by Opener

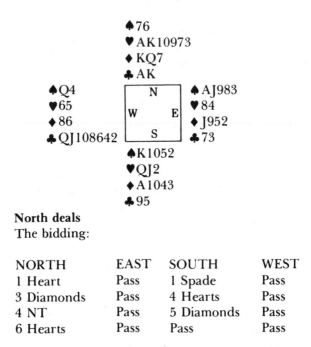

```
                    ♠76
                    ♥AK10973
                    ♦KQ7
                    ♣AK
     ♠Q4          ┌─────────┐      ♠AJ983
     ♥65          │    N    │      ♥84
     ♦86          │ W     E │      ♦J952
     ♣QJ108642    │    S    │      ♣73
                  └─────────┘
                    ♠K1052
                    ♥QJ2
                    ♦A1043
                    ♣95
```

North deals
The bidding:

NORTH	EAST	SOUTH	WEST
1 Heart	Pass	1 Spade	Pass
3 Diamonds	Pass	4 Hearts	Pass
4 NT	Pass	5 Diamonds	Pass
6 Hearts	Pass	Pass	Pass

North opened a Heart and South began the "11-12 Principle" with 1 Spade. North counted his hand at 21 and made a jump-shift to 3 Diamonds, forcing partner to bid again. South, delighted to do so, had to give a jump to show a Heart raise and bid 4. North diagnosed a slam and went into Blackwood; he found an Ace and bid 6.

East didn't have an attractive lead and settled on the Club 7.

Declarer counted six Heart tricks, three Diamonds and maybe four, two Clubs, maybe one Spade if the Ace was right = 11 sure's, two maybe's.

On the Club lead dummy played low, West followed with the 10 and declarer topped it with the King. He shifted to the trump King and then played a little Heart to the Queen, pulling in all the enemy trumps.

His next most promising suit was Diamonds so he played low to the King, took the Queen, and led low to the Ace. As West showed out the "maybe" in Diamonds went down the drain. Declarer led the Diamond 10 and trumped it. He took his Ace of Clubs. The moment arrived when he had to make the Spade play.

♠ 76

♠ K1052

He laid down the Spade 7, East ducked, and the Declarer reached for the King. It held! Then he ran his stream of trumps but East held onto the Spade Ace and took the 13th trick. North made his small slam by leading *toward* a King.

32. The 11-12 Principle

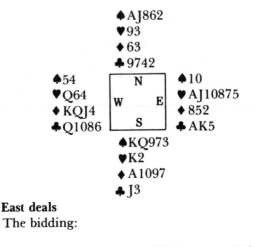

East deals
The bidding:

EAST	SOUTH	WEST	NORTH
1 Heart	1 Spade	2 Diamonds	2 Spades
3 Hearts	Pass	4 Hearts	Pass
Pass	Pass		

East opened a Heart and South overcalled his Spades. West's hand was worth 11 points so he bid a new suit, 2 Diamonds. North competed with 2 Spades. East rebid his long Hearts and West raised to 4. South started with the Spade King.

East held up the play a moment to count five Hearts, two Diamonds, and three Clubs = 10. He had little hope the Heart finesse would be successful with an overcall on his left.

Trick one went to South's Spade King with his partner encouraging with the 8. South continued the

Spade Queen and North completed the high-low signal with the 2 but declarer ruffed.

East went to the dummy with the Club Queen to lead the Queen of Hearts and let it ride. South covered with the King. He saw no desirable return so he continued a Heart which was won by declarer's 10. All the opponents' Hearts were in.

Declarer played the Club Ace and the Jack dropped. He took the King and shifted to a low Diamond. South saw no hope for another trick and went up with the Ace and returned a Diamond. Declarer took the King and Queen of Diamonds and had three trump winners in his hand, making his 4 Hearts.

South was right to stop leading his Spades. If he had continued them when he got in with his Heart King he would have given the declarer a ruff in dummy and a sluff in his hand. That's one of the No-No's in bridge.

IX. THE TWO-DEMAND

Some day you will pick up a hand with such a beautiful array of high cards that you can make a game even if your partner doesn't hold a face card. You don't want to open the bidding at the game level because you want to investigate slam possibilities. You might have two suits and want to ask your partner which one he likes better. Yet you cannot risk the hand being passed out. What can you do?

There is a special bid for such a hand. It's called the Two-Demand. It is just what the name implies. When you open the bidding with two of a suit it is a demand that your partner respond and *keep responding* until game is reached even with an empty hand.

It's the biggest bid in bridge and requires:

- 25 points with a good five-card suit,
- 23 points with a good six-card suit, or
- 21 points with a good seven-card suit.

Two five-card suits are worth a point.
If your suit is a minor you need two extra points.

On each of the following hands you would make an opening Two-Demand:

♠AKJxx	♥AKxxx	♦AQ	♣x
♠AKx	♥AKQxxx	♦AJx	♣x
♠AKJxxxx	♥AQ	♦Ax	♣xx

The first hand is worth 25 points (21 in high cards + 3 in distribution + 1 for the two-suiter). You want to be sure to reach game in Spades or Hearts but you don't know which one. You open 2 Spades, the higher ranking of two suits of the same length.

On the second you have 23 points (21 in high cards + 2 in distribution) and a good six-card suit. You're almost certain you want to play in Hearts but if your partner insisted on Spades or Diamonds you'd acquiesce. You also want to talk over slam possibilities. You open 2 Hearts.

On the third hand you have 21 points (18 high-card points + 3 distributional) and a strong seven-card suit. You're going to play this one in Spades but you want to consider a slam. You open 2 Spades.

Partner's Negative Response

Even if your partner has no points he will keep the bidding open for you. The negative response is 2 No Trump and shows zero to six points. It is artificial and has nothing to do with wanting to play No Trump. It says, "Don't count on me for points."

2 ♠ ☐ 2 NT shows 0-6 points

If your partner responds 2 No Trump the ball bounces back to you. What's your rebid? Make the bid that best describes your hand. On the first of the hands just discussed you would show your second suit and bid 3 Hearts. Now your partner will choose between your suits, bid a new suit, or rebid No Trump.

With the second hand you would rebid your six-card suit and say 3 Hearts. Again, your partner must keep the bidding open until you get to game.

On the third hand you have a self-sustaining trump suit. You know where you want to play this one. Say, "4 Spades".

With a Positive Response

Any response other than 2 No Trump is positive and shows a trick and a half — seven points or more — and is a slam invitation. The most encouraging bid is a raise promising three trumps.

Without a fit the bid of a new suit shows a holding at least as strong as QJxxx. A jump to 3 No Trump shows even distribution and scattered values.

As soon as a trump suit is agreed on the opener may want to check for Aces by using the Blackwood Convention to investigate the slam situation.

Opening 2 NT Isn't Forcing

Notice it is only the opening of 2 of a suit that demands a response. The opening bid of 2 No Trump shows 22 to 24 points and partner may pass with 0-3 points.

Flash Card

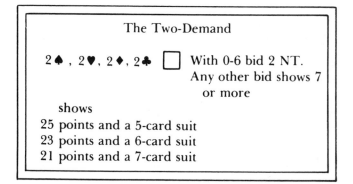

The Two-Demand

2♠ , 2♥, 2♦, 2♣ ☐ With 0-6 bid 2 NT.
Any other bid shows 7
or more

shows
25 points and a 5-card suit
23 points and a 6-card suit
21 points and a 7-card suit

IX. Two-Demand Bidding Drill

1. What's your point count and opening bid on the following:

♠AKQJ	♠AQxxx	♠AQJ	♠AKxx
♥AKxxx	♥AKQJ10	♥AKQxxxx	♥AKJx
♦Ax	♦Kx	♦Kx	♦x
♣Kx	♣A	♣x	♣AKxx
_____	_____	_____	_____

2. Partner opened 2 ♥   What would you respond?

♠QJ10xxx	♠xx	♠AKxxx	♠Kxx
♥x	♥QJx	♥xx	♥xx
♦xxx	♦Kxxx	♦10xx	♦Kxxx
♣xxx	♣Qxxx	♣xxx	♣Qxxx
_____	_____	_____	_____

3. Try bidding these hands until the auction is completed:

♠AKxxx	♠xx	♠AKQxxx	♠x
♥KQJxx	♥xxxx	♥AKx	♥QJxxx
♦Ax	♦xxx	♦- - -	♦xxxx
♣A	♣Kxxx	♣Axxx	♣xxx
Count _____	_____	_____	_____
1st bid _____	_____	_____	_____
Re-bid _____	_____	_____	_____

♠Ax	♠Kxx	♠AJx	♠Kxx
♥AKxxx	♥Qxxx	♥KQJ	♥xxx
♦KQJ	♦xxxxx	♦AKxx	♦J10x
♣AQJ	♣K	♣KJ10	♣xxxx
Count _____	_____	_____	_____
1st bid _____	_____	_____	_____
Re-bid _____	_____	_____	_____

33. The Two-Demand

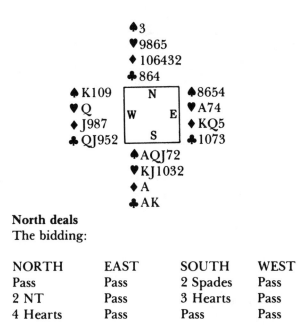

North deals
The bidding:

NORTH	EAST	SOUTH	WEST
Pass	Pass	2 Spades	Pass
2 NT	Pass	3 Hearts	Pass
4 Hearts	Pass	Pass	Pass

South judged his hand to be worth 26 points, 22 in high cards + 3 in ruffing value + 1 for two five-card suits and he made the exciting opening bid of 2 Spades. North had a bust but he kept the bidding alive with the negative bid of 2 No Trump. Now South suggested another suit, "3 Hearts". North raised to 4. South left it there; he couldn't consider a slam opposite a partner who was broke.

West led the Club Queen, the top of an imperfect sequence. Declarer took it with the King of Clubs.

South had two probable trump losers and three Spade losers. He needed to trump his losing Spades while dummy still had trumps so he postponed pulling trumps.

He cashed the Aces of Spades, led a baby Spade and trumped it in dummy. Now he played a Club to the Ace so he could lead another small Spade and trump it on the board. Lo, the King fell! Declarer's Spades were high.

Now he moved to extract the opponents' trumps leading the 9 of Hearts. East played low — the Ace of trumps is always a winner — and this gave West a chance possibly to capture an honor. Declarer finessed and West won the Queen of Hearts.

West returned the Jack of Clubs which South won with a trump. Declarer laid down the King of Hearts. East took the Ace and returned the Diamond King. Declarer came in with the Ace, pulled the last outstanding trump, and claimed the rest of the tricks, scoring five Hearts. He lost only two tricks, the Queen and the Ace of trumps.

34. Bidding a Slam

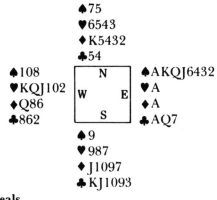

```
              ♠75
              ♥6543
              ♦K5432
              ♣54
   ♠108          N          ♠AKQJ6432
   ♥KQJ102    W     E       ♥A
   ♦Q86                     ♦A
   ♣862          S          ♣AQ7
              ♠9
              ♥987
              ♦J1097
              ♣KJ1093
```

East deals
The bidding:

EAST	SOUTH	WEST	NORTH
2 Spades	Pass	3 Hearts	Pass
4 NT	Pass	5 Clubs	Pass
5 NT	Pass	6 Diamonds	Pass
6 Spades	Pass	Pass	Pass

East counted 11 tricks in his own hand and opened 2 Spades. When West responded 3 Hearts, East started Blackwood with 4 No Trump. His partner said, "No Aces." Now, 5 No Trump. Yes, one King. East feared the Club suit and settled at 6 Spades.

South opened the Diamond Jack which rode to Declarer's Ace.

That was a beautiful 10 of Spades on the board, declarer's entry to the good Hearts. Declarer led the Ace of trumps, then the Ace of Hearts to unblock, and now back to trumps with a low one to dummy's 10, gathering in the last outstanding trump. He brought forth the King of Hearts and then the Queen, dropping the Club losers in the closed hand. Now the road was clear to bring in all 13 tricks.

35. A Positive Answer

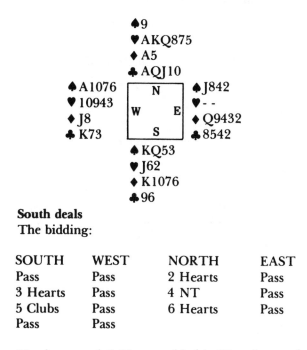

South deals
The bidding:

SOUTH	WEST	NORTH	EAST
Pass	Pass	2 Hearts	Pass
3 Hearts	Pass	4 NT	Pass
5 Clubs	Pass	6 Hearts	Pass
Pass	Pass		

North opened 2 Hearts with his 23 points and a strong six-card suit. His hand looked as if it could bring in a game with little or no help from his partner. South's two Kings and a Queen looked beautiful and he said, "3 Hearts". Now that trumps were agreed on North asked for Aces. When the answer was "zero" North parked at 6 Hearts.

East didn't want to lead into the slam hand but he finally laid down the Spade 2. Dummy's Queen came out and West captured the trick with the Ace and returned a little Spade. Declarer discarded a Club and won with dummy's King.

Declarer saw that all his cards were winners except he could lose to the Club King. He'd have to finesse twice and needed two entries to dummy.

He led low to the Heart Ace and East failed to follow. Now the Heart King was played and next a baby Heart to the Jack.

The Club 9 came off the board and declarer finessed the Jack and it won. Declarer remembered there was still a Heart outstanding and led the Queen to bring it in.

Now a Diamond to the King to get the lead back in dummy. The Club 6 was played and the Queen inserted. It won. Declarer took the Club Ace, the Diamond Ace, and had two trumps to claim his slam.

36. Opening 2 No Trump

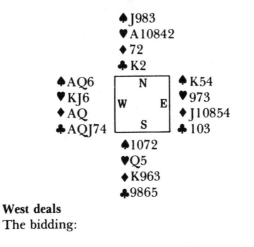

```
                    ♠ J983
                    ♥ A10842
                    ♦ 72
                    ♣ K2
        ♠ AQ6                      ♠ K54
        ♥ KJ6         N            ♥ 973
        ♦ AQ       W     E         ♦ J10854
        ♣ AQJ74       S            ♣ 103
                    ♠ 1072
                    ♥ Q5
                    ♦ K963
                    ♣ 9865
```

West deals
The bidding:

WEST	NORTH	EAST	SOUTH
2 NT	Pass	3 NT	Pass
Pass	Pass		

West bid 2 No Trump announcing a specific holding of 22-24 high card points and a balanced hand. Was East forced to bid? No, but with four points he voted for game.

All No Trump openers show a limited number of points, 1 NT = 16-18, 2 NT = 22-24, and 3 NT = 25-27.

North led the fourth best of his longest and strongest suit, the Heart 4, South pushed with the Queen, and West took the King.

West studied his two long suits, seven Clubs and seven Diamonds. Which should he develop? He had to keep South out of the lead; he didn't want South leading through his Heart holding. He didn't have the entries to dummy to work on Diamonds so he chose Clubs. If the Club King was on his right he might get five Clubs, one Diamond, one Heart, and three Spades = 10.

The Club play had to be made from the board so declarer led to dummy's Spade King. He then pulled out the Club 10 and let it go. North took his King. He exited with a Club, waiting for someone else to lead Hearts to him.

Declarer ran four Club tricks, cashed the Ace and Queen of Spades, and took his Ace of Diamonds to make his ninth trick. Then he led the Diamond Queen. South took his King and led his carefully preserved Heart 5 for his partner who came in with his Ace and 10 of Hearts.

Tips:

Some new players have a difficult time remembering what suit partner led. When you become more experienced it will engrave itself on your memory. Until then, try an old trick from the days of Whist. As soon as your partner makes the opening lead rearrange your cards, moving your partner's suit to the extreme left of your hand.

A Two-Demand is forcing to game unless an opponent overcalls and either partner doubles for penalties.

After a Two-Demand the responder with a borderline hand of five or six points and a trump fit makes the normal negative response of 2 No Trump but later may jump.

2 ♠		2 NT
3 ♠		5 ♠

The opener may accept this slam invitation by bidding 6 or decline by passing.

X. THE PREEMPTIVE BID

A preemptive bid is a call of 3, 4, or 5 in a suit and describes a hand with a long suit of seven or more cards but few high cards — not more than 9 or 10 points, most of which are concentrated in the trump suit.

It's a strategic maneuver to rob the enemy of bidding space. They have to enter the auction at a high level; they're going to have difficulty exchanging information about their point count and distribution. They have to guess and they might guess wrong, landing in the wrong suit and going down; or they might bid a game and miss a slam.

Is it dangerous? No, your long trump suit is a safety valve. Occasionally an unkind Fate will stack the trump suit against you and you'll suffer a big penalty when the opponents had no game. Don't be discouraged. There will be many more hands when the opponents will be placed at a disadvantage and your preempt will gain handsomely.

It's a defensive bid. With an opening hand an orthodox bid of one is preferred.

The Rule of Two or Three

There's a formula to help you decide when and how much to preempt. It's the "Rule of Two or Three". Count your tricks and bid two more than you have if you're vulnerable and three more than you have if you're not vulnerable. This is to protect you from losing more than 500 if you get doubled and go down.

♠8   ♥KQJ76532   ♦87   ♣85

Here you have seven tricks if Hearts are trumps. If you're vulnerable you overbid by two (7 + 2 = 9) so you open 3 Hearts. If you're not vulnerable you overbid by three (7 + 3 = 10) and you open 4 Hearts.

Counting Tricks

There is a way to help you count your tricks. After the first three leads of a long suit like the Heart suit above, the opponents will probably be out of Hearts so all your little ones will take tricks. So, draw an imaginary line after the third card in your suit:

$$♥KQJ/76532$$

Count each card on the right of the line a trick; now figure how many tricks you can expect on the left of the line. Here are some examples:

♠AJ107654   ♥7   ♦QJ10   ♣76

♠7   ♥KJ107643   ♦K54   ♣76

♠A   ♥764   ♦AQJ6543   ♣98

♠K765432   ♥87   ♦K75   ♣4

In the first hand, the AJ10 will usually bring in two tricks, plus four small cards, plus one for the ♦QJ10 equals seven tricks, so open 4 Spades not vulnerable and 3 Spades vulnerable.

On the second hand, the KJ10 is one and a half tricks (depending on who has the Queen) so this is worth five and a half tricks plus a half in Diamonds. (Sometimes you'll get a trick with the King and sometimes you won't.) That's six tricks so open 3 Hearts not vulnerable and pass vulnerable.

The third hand is too good for a preempt with the outside Ace and 11 high card points. With distribution it's worth 14. Open 1 Diamond.

On the last the King is half a trick, plus four little cards, plus a half for the Diamond King. That's five, not enough. You pass.

Avoid a preempt when your partner hasn't bid and you have support in a major because you might miss a game in that major:

♠QJ42   ♥7   ♦8   ♣KQJ9853

In Third Seat

Sitting in third position your partner has already passed and a preempt can be made with greater flexibility.

♠5   ♥KJ76532   ♦65   ♣742

You have only four high-card points. There are 36 points outstanding. Your partner couldn't bid, your right-hand opponent couldn't bid. The fourth hand has lots of points. Not vulnerable open 3 Hearts although you can't provide your quota of tricks.

Responding to a Preempt

Most often when your partner preempts, you will pass. Sometimes your partner will make an opening preempt and you will have a good hand. You are in the happy position of knowing how many tricks your partner has. Add yours to his. If you're vulnerable and he bid 3 Hearts, he has seven tricks. You need three to go to game. These should be quick tricks, Aces and Kings. With your partner's distribution Queens and Jacks won't help much. You have:

♠A764   ♥9   ♦KQ76   ♣AK72

If you feel a strong urge to bid 3 No Trump suppress that temptation. Your partner's Heart suit probably isn't solid. To make a game in No Trump the responder to a preempt should have a reasonable prospect of nine tricks in his own hand.

With your four quick tricks bid 4 Hearts. Don't worry about the singleton Heart. The preempter probably has seven and that one makes the eight needed for a trump suit.

The same hand minus the Ace and King of Clubs has only two tricks, partner's 7 + your 2 = 9. Pass.

Your Opponents Preempt

When your opponents make an opening preempt and you want to bid you need a strong hand to come in, 16 points or more including distribution. If you have a suit, you can overcall. If you have points but no suit, you can double to ask partner to name the suit. Some players won't enter the bidding when it is so high. Others are egged on because they think someone is trying to steal something from them. The biggest swings in score at bridge are caused by preemptive bids even in expert circles.

Responding to a Take-out Double

When your partner doubles a preempt and asks you to bid remember to jump with 10 points just as you would with the double of an opening one bid.

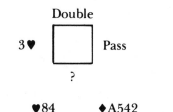

With this hand bid 4 Spades. Without one of the Aces bid 3 Spades.

Flash Card

A Preemptive Bid

Opening 3 or more of a suit:

Seven-card suit or longer
Not more than 10 high-card points
Overbid by two tricks vulnerable,
three tricks not vulnerable.

Tips:

The preempter never bids again. His partner, knowing so much about the hand, makes all future decisions.

You can make a preemptive overcall also:

1♥

 3♠

You also show a preemptive hand with a single jump:

1♥

 2♠

Sometimes preemptive bids are made on a six-card suit.

X. Preemptive Drill

1. What would you open non-vulnerable with:

♠82	♠KJ98765	♠87	♠K54
♥AKQ1042	♥J	♥63	♥10
♦10842	♦QJ10	♦AKJ8743	♦AQJ10972
♣8	♣43	♣64	♣K3

2. Your partner opened 3 Clubs not-vulnerable. What do you bid with:

♠A1042	♠AK7643	♠KQJ10976	♠AK3
♥AJ74	♥KJ75	♥AK	♥AQ2
♦A974	♦73	♦8	♦KQJ962
♣3	♣7	♣642	♣7

3. Your partner opened 3 Hearts vulnerable. What do you bid with:

♠AK72	♠AK10762	♠K32	♠AKQ10
♥8	♥KJ2	♥A42	♥K
♦AQJ2	♦- - -	♦K652	♦AK6543
♣A742	♣K652	♣652	♣A3

4. Your right-hand opponent opened 3 Diamonds, not-vulnerable. What do you bid with:

♠7	♠K764	♠AQJ3	♠AQJ763
♥AJ32	♥QJ96	♥K1092	♥4
♦AK765	♦5	♦9	♦A52
♣875	♣AJ72	♣AQ104	♣K73

37. The Preemptive Bid

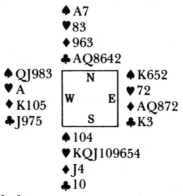

```
              ♠ A7
              ♥ 83
              ♦ 963
              ♣ AQ8642
  ♠ QJ983      ┌─────────┐   ♠ K652
  ♥ A          │    N    │   ♥ 72
  ♦ K105       │ W     E │   ♦ AQ872
  ♣ J975       │    S    │   ♣ K3
               └─────────┘
              ♠ 104
              ♥ KQJ109654
              ♦ J4
              ♣ 10
```

South deals

The bidding, E-W vulnerable:

SOUTH	WEST	NORTH	EAST
4 Hearts	Pass	Pass	Pass

North and South hadn't scored on the rubber and the opponents had a game when South picked up these cards. He longed for a good hand. Only six high-card points! Then he studied his beautiful Heart suit. If Hearts were trumps he could take seven tricks. He preempted 4 Hearts. West passed, North passed, and East squirmed in his chair but he didn't dare enter the auction at this level with a minimum opener.

West led the Spade Queen and declarer took the Ace as East encouraged with the Spade 6. South tackled trumps right away, leading dummy's Heart 8. West won the Ace and cashed his Spade Jack. Then he shifted to a low Diamond. East rose with the Ace and returned a little Diamond. West took the Diamond King and continued the suit. Declarer trumped.

Immediately, South led the Heart King to bring in the last outstanding trump. Then he took the Ace of Clubs. Now he laid down his hand which was all trumps and claimed the rest of the tricks. He was down one and East-West scored 50 points.

Without South's preemptive bid the opponents would have found their 4 Spade contract. Their values were divided and neither was strong enough to come in at such a high level.

38. Raising a Preempt

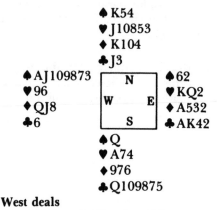

```
              ♠ K54
              ♥ J10853
              ♦ K104
              ♣ J3
♠ AJ109873    ┌─────────┐    ♠ 62
♥ 96          │    N    │    ♥ KQ2
♦ QJ8         │ W     E │    ♦ A532
♣ 6           │    S    │    ♣ AK42
              └─────────┘
              ♠ Q
              ♥ A74
              ♦ 976
              ♣ Q109875
```

West deals

The bidding, E-W vulnerable:

WEST	NORTH	EAST	SOUTH
3 Spades	Pass	4 Spades	Pass
Pass	Pass		

West preempted 3 Spades vulnerable announcing a long suit and seven tricks. East held four quick tricks in Aces and Kings and happily bid game.

North led the Jack of Hearts, declarer covered with dummy's Queen and South captured it with the Ace. South returned the Heart 7, declarer played the 9, North covered with the 10, and dummy's King won.

West counted five or six Spade winners, two Clubs, two Diamonds, and the Heart he'd already won = 10 or 11. However, his possible losers were four, the King and Queen of Spades, the King of Diamonds, and he had already lost the Ace of Hearts. He hoped to avoid one loser.

Declarer started with a baby Spade from dummy, South dropped the Queen, and West took his Ace. One loser had been eliminated.

He led the Spade Jack and North took the King. Now North laid down the high 8 of Hearts but West ruffed it and led the Spade 10 to pick up the last outstanding trump.

He played the Diamond Queen planning to finesse but North covered with the King and forced dummy's Ace. Another loser eliminated. He continued a Diamond back to the Jack.

Then declarer led the Club 6 to the Ace on the board, and continued with the Club King on which he discarded the losing 8 of Diamonds from the closed hand. He showed his three high trumps and claimed the rest. He brought in 11 tricks.

39. The Preemptive Overcall

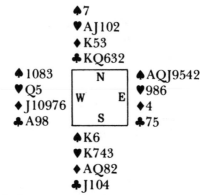

```
              ♠7
              ♥AJ102
              ♦K53
              ♣KQ632
   ♠1083      ┌─────────┐   ♠AQJ9542
   ♥Q5        │    N    │   ♥986
   ♦J10976    │ W     E │   ♦4
   ♣A98       │    S    │   ♣75
              └─────────┘
              ♠K6
              ♥K743
              ♦AQ82
              ♣J104
```

North deals

The bidding, none vulnerable:

NORTH	EAST	SOUTH	WEST
1 Club	3 Spades	?	

North opened 1 Club and East preempted 3 Spades throwing a monkey wrench into the bidding machinery. Now what could South do with his opening hand? Try a treacherous 3 No Trump? (How could North-South find their Heart fit at this level?)

Against 3 Spades doubled, a possible contract, South opened the Jack of Clubs and declarer went up with dummy's Ace.

Declarer could find only eight tricks to count, six Spades, one Club, and a Heart ruff.

He led the Spade 10 and finessed but South came in with the King and won. South returned the Club 10 which won. He continued the 4 of Clubs and North played the Queen but declarer stepped in with a trump.

East led the Spade Ace to pull the last trump from the enemy and exited with his singleton Diamond. South picked up the Queen and continued the Ace but East walked out with a trump again.

Now declarer exited with a low Heart. South won the King and continued a small Heart to North's Ace. The next Heart was trumped in dummy and then declarer played the three trumps in his hand. The contract was down one.

4 Heart Contract

Now let's see how things would go if East passed and South landed in 4 Hearts. West would open the Jack of Diamonds and South would take the Queen.

Now he would play the King of Hearts and continue a low one. West's Queen would drop and dummy's Ace would win. Now the Jack of Hearts would bring in the trump suit.

Declarer would move to set up his next best suit, leading a low Club to the 10, taken by West's Ace. West would switch to a Spade and East would take the Ace and continue the Spade Queen. Declarer would win the King, take the Jack of Clubs, now over to the King and Queen of Clubs. Now he'd take the King and Ace of Diamonds, and have a trump trick left to make 5 Hearts!

40. Finding a Slam

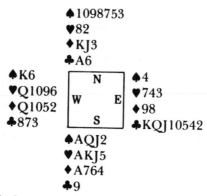

```
              ♠1098753
              ♥82
              ♦KJ3
              ♣A6
  ♠K6                        ♠4
  ♥Q1096        N            ♥743
  ♦Q1052     W     E         ♦98
  ♣873          S            ♣KQJ10542
              ♠AQJ2
              ♥AKJ5
              ♦A764
              ♣9
```

East deals

The bidding (none vulnerable):

EAST	SOUTH	WEST	NORTH
3 Clubs	Double	Pass	4 Spades
Pass	4 NT	Pass	5 Diamonds
Pass	5 NT	Pass	6 Diamonds
Pass	6 Spades	Pass	Pass
Pass			

East counted six tricks in his Club suit and pre-empted 3 Clubs. South made a take-out double. With a long major and a hand that valued at 10 points North jumped to 4 Spades. Now South saw a possible slam and asked his partner how many Aces he had. The answer was one. With all the Aces accounted for South asked for Kings. Partner had only one and South signed off with 6 Spades.

East opened the King of Clubs which was topped by declarer's Ace. North saw two possible losers, the King of Spades and Queen of Diamonds. He led the 10 of Spades and tried the trump finesse but West showed up with the King. He returned a Club and let dummy trump.

North called in the last trump by playing the Ace. Now he cashed the Ace of Hearts and the King of Hearts. He pulled out a low Heart and trumped it in his hand. He hoped the Queen would fall so he could discard a Diamond on the good Jack of Hearts but it didn't. Now he'd have to take the Diamond finesse.

He played a Diamond to the Ace and returned a Diamond finessing the Jack which held the trick. He cashed the King of Diamonds and had three trumps left to score the little slam. He tried two finesses, lost one and won the other.

ANSWERS for DRILLS

I. Opening 1 NT and Responses

1. No, 19   Yes, 16   No (uneven   No, 17
                         distribution), 17
2. Pass, 6   2 NT, 8   3 NT, 10
3. Pass.   3 NT   3 NT
4. Q spades   6 spades   K spades

II. Bidding One Spade or One Heart

1. 16+2, 1H   11+3, 1S   16, 1 NT
   12, Pass   17+3, 1H
2. Pass   2H   3H
3. 4S   Pass   4S

III. Bidding One Club or One Diamond

1. 14+1, 1D   14+1, 1C   16, 1 NT   19+1, 1C
2. 6+1, 1H   16+1, 1S   10+2, 1D   12+2, 1H
3. 4H   2H   1S   2C
4. 2S   3S   2C   2D

IV. The Overcall

1. 1S   Pass   Pass   1 NT   2D
2. 9+1, 2S   12+1, 3S   Pass
3. 8+1, 2H   9, 1 NT   14+1, 3H

V. Slam Bidding

1. 33   26   29   37
2. 6 NT   6 NT   7 NT
3. 4 NT   4 NT   4S
4. 5H   6H   5 NT

VI. Suit Responses to 1 NT

1.	17, 1D	18, 1 NT	17, 1C	19, 1C
2.	2 NT	4S	3S	2H rescue
	Pass	3 NT		
3.	4H	3 NT	4H	

VII. The Take-out Double

1.	1S	Double	Double	Pass
	2D	Double		
2.	Double	1S	1S	
3.	1H (or 1S)	2S	1 NT	4H

VIII. Major Suit Responses

1.	7+1, 2H	10+2, 2C	7, 1 NT	7+4, 4H
2.	2H, min.	2C min.	2S, min.	2 NT, max.
	3 NT, max.	3C, max.	1 NT min.	2D, min.
	2D, med.	3S, med.	3H, med.	

IX. The Two-Demand

1.	24+2, 2H	23+4, 2S	19+3, 2H	22+2, 1C
2.	2 NT	3H	2S	3 NT
3.	21+1+3	3+1	20+3	3+2
	2S	2 NT	2S	2 NT
	3H	4H	3S	4H
			Pass	

24+1	9	22	4
2H	3H	2 NT	3 NT
4 NT	5C	Pass	
6H			

X. Preemptive Drill

1. 3H	3S	4D	1D
2. Pass	Pass	4S	3 NT
3. 4H	6H (or 4 NT)	Pass	4 NT
4. Pass	Pass	Double	3S

BASIC REFERENCE CHARTS

BIDDING SUMMARY

The Point Count System

Ace	 4	Void	 3
King	 3	Singleton	 2
Queen	 2	Doubleton	 1
Jack	 1	Unprotected honor -1	
All 4 Aces	 1	Opener with no Aces -1.	

Needed for Game

26 points = 3 No Trump, 4♠ , 4♥
29 points = 5♣ or 5♦
33 points = 6 (a small slam)
37 points = 7 (a grand slam)

The No Trump Story

High cards only, even distribution

1 NT = 16-18   2 NT = 22-24   3 NT = 25-27

Responding to 1 NT with Even Distribution

1 No Trump ☐   with 0-7 pass
  16-18   with 8-9 bid 2 NT (inviting 3)
                             with 10-14 bid 3 NT
                             with 15-16 bid 4 NT (inviting 6)
                             with 17-18 bid 6 NT
                             with 19-20 bid 5 NT (Partner bids 6
                                 NT with a minimum, 7 NT with
                                 a maximum)
                             with 21 bid 7 NT

Responding with a Long Suit

1 NT ☐ With 0-7 and a 5- or 6-card suit rescue with
               2♦ , 2♥ or 2♠
           With 10 and a 6-card major jump to 4♥ or
               4♠
           With 10 and a 5-card major jump to 3♥ or
               3♠
           Conceal a long minor. With 8-9 bid 2 NT;
               with 10 bid 3 NT

THE OPENING SUIT BID

When you open the bidding 1 Club, 1 Diamond, 1 Heart, or 1 Spade you show 13 to 21 in high-card points and distribution, a wide range. If partner responds you choose a rebid that brings your hand more sharply into focus.

REBIDS BY OPENER

With 13-15 Minimum Opener

Pass if your partner raised your suit to 2.

Raise partner's suit to 2 with 4-card support.

Name a new 4-card suit at the 1 level.

Name a new suit at the 2 level *lower* in rank than your first suit.

Rebid your suit if it's a good five-card suit or longer.

Bid 1 No Trump with even distribution.

With 16-18 Medium Opener

Bid 3 if your partner raised your suit to 2.

Jump raise partner with four-card support.

Name a new four-card suit at the 1 level.

Name a new suit at the 2 level *lower* in rank than your first suit.

Jump in your original suit with six cards and a good suit.

With 19-21 Maximum Opener

Jump to game if partner raised your major to 2.

Jump to game in partner's major with four cards in it.

Jump in a new suit, forcing to game.

Reverse, a rebid at the 2 level in a suit higher in rank than the one originally named (You, 1 Club; Partner, 1 Spade; You, 2 Hearts). Forcing.

Jump to 2 NT with a balanced hand and 19 points.

Jump to 3 NT with a balanced hand and 20-21.

RESPONDING TO A SUIT

When your partner opens the bidding with 1 of a suit you choose the response which gives the best picture of your hand:

With 6-10 points, A Weak Hand

Raise partner's major to 2 with three trumps.

Jump partner's major to game with five trumps, a void or a singleton, no more than 9 high-card points.

Name a new four-card suit at the 1 level.

Respond 1 No Trump without trump support.

With 11-12, A Good Hand Worth Two Bids

Name a new suit at the lowest level; after partner rebids, make a second response.

With 13-15(16), You See Game

Jump raise partner's major with four trumps, or three with an honor.

Name a new suit and later move toward game. Tip: The only way to force opener to bid again is to name a new suit, or jump the bidding below the game level.

Jump to 2 No Trump with even distribution, protection in the other suits.

With (16)17-18, Think About a Slam

With support for partner's suit, bid two new suits, and then give partner a jump raise. With a good 5-card suit, jump shift in your suit. If opener shows a minimum, stop at game.

Name a new four-card suit at the 1 level.

Without trump support jump to 3 No Trump with a balanced hand, protection in other suits.

With 19 or more, A Slam Hand

Jump the bidding in a good five-card suit, or make forcing bids to the slam level.

When a trump suit is discovered use the Blackwood convention.

OPENING LEADS

Top of a sequence in honors:

K̲QJ   Q̲J10   K̲QJ1075   1̲0984

Exception: AK̲4

With a single honor lead 4th best (or 3rd if you only have three) which says, "Partner, please return."

K762̲   Q543̲   J72̲

Top of nothing which says, "Partner, don't return."

9̲73   8̲63   7̲52

Top of a doubleton:

J̲2   9̲4   .   A̲K   A̲7

●*Against No Trump* contracts lead the 4th best of your longest and strongest suit *unless* you have a sequence in honors, when you lead the top:

AJ742̲   KJ432̲   K̲QJ43   K̲Q73̲   K̲Q107

If your partner bid a suit lead his suit using the rules above.

●*Against a suit* contract:

    Two is a sequence: K̲Q42   J̲1082
    Avoid leading from a "tenace": K̲J3   Q102
    Don't lead from an Ace; declarer might have the singleton King and make it: A72̲   No!

If your partner bid a suit, lead his suit using the rules above. Exception: if you have the Ace lead it.

Lead 1) your partner's suit, 2) the top of a sequence in honors, or 3) an unbid suit. Leading to the first trick is the most difficult play in bridge. These are a few guideposts.

Dummy Points

When you have support in your partner's suit you promote one trump honor one point, Kxx is 4, QJx is 4. Don't promote any if you already have 4 points in trumps, KJx remains 4. Don't promote an Ace.

Distributional points are more valuable: Void is 5, Singleton is 3, Doubleton is still 1.

Elementary Card Combinations

Finesses

All of these plays will create a trick for you 50% of the time because half the time the crucial card is dealt to your left-hand opponent and half the time to your right-hand opponent. If you always finesse, half the time you'll win.

Finessing for a King

Your Hand   Dummy
   AQ2 653
                         Trying to win two tricks, lead low from dummy, if next hand plays low put in the Queen.

   A63 ☐ QJ10
                         To win three tricks lead the Queen and let it ride if it isn't covered by the King. Repeat with the Jack.

Finessing for a Queen

   AKJ ☐ 732
                         To win three tricks play the Ace then go to dummy in another suit and lead low to the Jack.

   AJ3 ☐ K42
                         To win three tricks play the King and then lead low to the Jack.

A102 ☐ KJ3   To win three tricks play the Ace and low to the Jack, or the King and low to the 10, depending on who you think has the Queen.

Leading Toward an Honor

Your Hand   Dummy
42 ☐ K5   To win one trick lead low from your hand and if the next player follows low go up with the King.

542 ☐ KQ6   To win two tricks lead low from your hand and play the King. If it wins return to your hand in another suit and lead low to the Queen.

A54 ☐ Q63   To win two tricks play the Ace and lead low to the Queen. If second hand plays a low card go up with the Queen.

A54 ☐ Q6   To win two tricks lead low toward the Queen. Do not play the Ace first.

Scoring Drill

Last night when you played bridge the first eight hands were these. Score them.

1. WE bid 1 NT and made 2.
2. THEY bid 3 Spades and went down 1.
3. THEY bid 4 Hearts and made 5.
4. WE bid 6 Clubs and made it. The declarer's trump holding was AKJ1072.
5. THEY bid 2 Spades and made 3.
6. WE bid 4 Diamonds, were doubled, and went down 2.
7. THEY bid 2 Hearts, were doubled, and went down 3.
8. THEY bid 2 Spades, were doubled, and made 3.

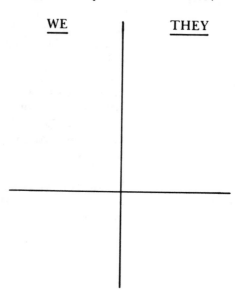

WE	THEY

Answer: WE + 1640, and THEY + 1610

hand to you. Bridge is a partnership game and only your partner can help you reach the best contract. The one who deals the cards has the privilege of making the first bid and the bidding continues clockwise around the table.

In the bidding the four suits rank alphabetically. Clubs are the lowest, then Diamonds, Hearts, and Spades.

♠ Spade

♥ Heart

♦ Diamond

♣ Club

Outranking all four suits is the bid of No Trump. As the name implies a No Trump contract is played without a trump suit. More contracts are played at No Trump than at any other denomination.

If you open the bidding with 1 Club the next player may, if he wishes, bid any suit at the 1 level because each suit outranks Clubs. However, if you opened 1 Spade any player who wants to bid a suit must go to the 2 level because Spades rank highest.

When you have no bid to make you say, "Pass". When three players in succession have said pass, the last bid gets the contract.

The Play of the Cards

Then the play of the cards begins. The object is to win tricks. A trick is the play of a card by each person

MECHANICS FOR THE BEGINNER

It takes four players for contract bridge, two pairs of partners who sit opposite each other at the table.

To determine the partnership, a deck of cards is fanned out face down. Each player chooses a card. The two drawing the highest are partners and the two drawing the lowest are partners. The player drawing the highest card wins the right to deal first, to choose the deck he wishes, and to choose the chair he likes.

The player to the left of the dealer shuffles the cards two or three times and then presents them to the dealer who asks the player on his right to cut the deck in two piles. The dealer places the bottom heap on top. He deals first to the player on his left, then clockwise around the table, one card at a time, until all the cards are distributed.

During the deal the dealer's partner shuffles another deck so it will be ready for the next dealer. The deal rotates clockwise so the unused deck, when shuffled, is placed at the left of the next dealer.

There are two parts to bridge, the bidding or auction to see which side will win the contract, and then the play of the cards.

The Bidding

The object of the bidding is to describe your hand to your partner and to have your partner describe his in this book. After your fourth class you'll be ready to go out on your own. It will be good for your bridge to play once a week. It's like swimming; you have to get in the water to learn.

There are 40,000,000 bridge players in this country and 1,000,000 taking lessons. You're going to have lots of people to play with. Good players are in great demand. The better you play the happier your friends will be to play with you.

The story goes that one night at the White House Lynda Byrd Johnson needed a fourth for bridge and sent out to see if one of the Presidential aides could play. A Captain Charles Robb appeared. The captain played well and he was invited to play again. He was even taken on the Presidential yacht, the Sequoia, to play with the First Lady, Mrs. Lyndon Johnson. Soon the captain and Lynda Byrd were dating, became engaged, and were married.

I hope you find lots of friends and many hours of pleasure playing my favorite card game.

Caroline Sydnor

FOREWORD

This bridge book is for people who have seldom if ever played contract bridge and for people who have been "playing" all their lives and would like to learn scientific bidding.

I remember so well one of my students, Syd, who had "played" for 20 years. In his second lesson he opened the bidding with 1 Spade and his partner jumped to 3 Spades.

"Isn't it great," Syd said in wonder, "to know what your partner has when he bids." It was a marvel to Syd's partners also as they learned they could depend on his bids.

So come along with me (I hope you have a teacher to guide you) and we'll learn point-count bidding. This book explains 10 fundamental bids and responses and a dozen card plays that crop up most frequently.

This is Standard American bidding, the most popular system in the United States, played by 85 per cent of our tournament players. You can move to San Francisco or Dallas and find people playing the same system. It's founded on a strong opening No Trump of 16 to 18 high card points and opening five-card majors, the modern way to play bridge.

You'll play hands in your first class. With a deck of Caroline's Cards very quickly you can deal the 40 hands

In 1904 competitive bidding began and the name became Auction Bridge.

Harold Vanderbilt set out in 1926 to add the ceiling principle of a French game, Plafond, where only tricks contracted for counted toward a game and a slam bonus.

He gathered a Bridge foursome and took a nine-day ocean voyage through the Panama Canal to test his idea. All were fascinated with his "Contract" Bridge. He compiled a new scoring table using the decimal system, increased trick and game values, and added vulnerability. Returning to New York he gave typed copies of his innovations to several Auction Bridge friends and made no other effort to popularize his "Contract" Bridge. "It popularized itself," he declared, "and spread like wildfire."

He mentioned the game often in his letters and recorded occasional losses in his detailed account books. He lost small sums to Anne Washington, the wife of Major Lawrence Washington, twice in February of 1749 at Belvoir. Again he listed losses to Ann Spearing of 4/6, 3/9, and 1/6* in the spring of 1755. Martha might have been the better player; he noted only one time when she was behind and her loss, only 1/3**.

In 1742 the *Virginia Magazine* carried an article on the Whist vogue and asserted that some gentlemen and ladies were playing six evenings a week.

In Washington's Whist all four hands were concealed which made the play of the cards much more difficult than it is today. Nevertheless, their card play was highly refined and after 200 years we still teach many plays exactly as they made them. In this book which gives twelve plays, four of them were handed down to us from Whist, including the Bath Coup, presumed to be named after the English watering place of Bath.

Modern bidding, however, was unknown to them and the trump suit was determined by turning face up the last card dealt.

After Washington's day the game changed slightly and the dealer was accorded the privilege of naming the trump suit. By 1880 the dealer, if he chose, could "bridge" this decision over to his partner and the name became Bridge-Whist. A new contract of "No Trump" was added and one hand was exposed during the play as the "dummy".

---

* In today's currency about $11.20, $9.30, and $3.70, respectively.
** About $3.10.

HOW WHIST BECAME BRIDGE
1776 to 1976

George Washington played bridge and he called it Whist. Our forefathers brought the popular card game with them when they sailed from England where it was a national pastime in the 17th century.

It was so commonly known in Britain that it was said "every child almost of eight years hath a competent knowledge in that recreation."

A book describing card plays was written in London in 1743 and instantly became a best-seller; it was the first scientific study of a card game. The author, a little-known barrister, Edmond Hoyle, was quoted so frequently at the card table that the phrase "according to Hoyle" became an international idiom.

Reprinted many times, even pirated in one country, Hoyle's treatise was carried across the Atlantic and circulated in the American Colonies. Surely it was in the library at Mount Vernon where the revelry of Whist was a popular addition to Martha Washington's frequent dinner parties.

George Washington liked to play the game and in January of 1758, with a note of urgency, he ordered from England:
> "A neat maha'y Card Table
> 2 doz'n Packs of play'g Cards by the
> first Vessel."

How to Keep Score

There are three ways to get a big score. Win a rubber, bid and make a slam, and double the opponents and set them.

The rubber bonus is for winning two games: 700 for a two-game rubber, 500 for a three game rubber.

Only tricks contracted for count toward game and are scored below the line. Every thing else goes above the line.

Trick score: ♠ and ♥,   30 a trick
                ♦ and ♣,   20 a trick
                No Trump,   40 the 1st trick
                                  30 for all others

A game is 100 points. You don't have to get it all in one deal. You may score 40 ("a leg") on the first hand and 60 on another. Whenever a game is scored any "leg" is cut off.

You are vulnerable when you have a game.

	Not Vulnerable	**Vul.**
A small slam (12 tricks)	bid & made 500	750
A grand slam (13 tricks)	bid & made 1000	1500

Setting the Opponents

	Vul.	**Dbld.**	**Vul. & Dbld.**
First trick ...	50 ..100	100	200
Each additional	50 ..100	200	300

Redoubled: multiply by two

Fulfilling a Doubled Contract

Trick score below the line is doubled.
Overtricks made when doubled 100, Vul. 200.
Redoubled: multiply by two.
For making a doubled contract   50

Trump Honors: 4 in one hand, 100; 5 in one hand 150; 4 Aces in one hand at NT, 150.